THE
SPIRIT
OF
CHRIST

THE SPIRIT OF CHRIST

Mariano Di Gangi

A CANON PRESS BOOK

BAKER BOOK HOUSE
Grand Rapids, Michigan

CONTENTS

Preface 7

1 The Masterpiece 9

2 Descent of the Dove 17

3 Encounter in the Wilderness 27

4 The Lord's Anointed 41

5 Secret of Sacred Joy 49

6 Jesus: David's Son
    or Satan's Son? 57

7 Eternal Redemption 67

8 A Matter of Death and Life 77

9 To Glorify Christ 87

10 Apocalyptic Epilogue 97

PREFACE

New Testament Christianity is both kerygmatic and charismatic. The *charismata,* or gifts of the Spirit, are given to advance the cause of the *kerygma,* or gospel message. Spiritual gifts are not given for mere personal enjoyment, much less for ego inflation, but for service and witness. They are imparted to enlighten and empower us so that we may faithfully present Him in whose person the Spirit was at work for the defeat of the devil and the deliverance of His people.

Abraham Kuyper remarked in *The Work of the Holy Spirit*: "The Church has never sufficiently confessed the influence of the Holy Spirit exerted upon the work of Christ. The general impression is that the work of the Holy Spirit begins when the work of the Mediator on earth is finished. . . . Yet the Scripture teaches us again and again that Christ performed His mediatorial work controlled and impelled by the Holy Spirit."

Jesus was conceived of the Spirit and born of the virgin Mary. He was anointed with the Spirit to fulfill His calling as the Messiah and abounded in the fruit of the Spirit. By the Spirit's power He dealt decisively with the demonic element, whether alone as in the wilderness or in confrontation with demons within the personalities of men. By the Spirit He offered Himself to God in redeeming sacrifice, and by that same Spirit He was raised from the dead.

We may experience the presence of the Spirit of Christ creating life analogous to the life of Christ within us. We can be reborn by the Spirit and receive His anointing. We can be filled with the Spirit, endowed with His power so productive of godliness. It is by the Spirit that we offer to God that living sacrifice which is our free, reasonable, spiritual service. By the Spirit we shall be raised from the dead at the last.

7

1

THE MASTERPIECE

Matthew 1:18-25

The New Testament is like a gallery of art. We enter this gallery and begin in the Matthean wing. There are many miniature portraits of men such as Abraham, Isaac, Jacob, and Judah. We scan the pictures of David, Solomon, Rehoboam, Abijah, Asa, and Jehoshaphat. We see Uzziah, Hezekiah, Manasseh, Amon, and Josiah. We pause a while before Joseph and Mary. But then our attention is directed to the masterpiece titled *Immanuel* that is the work of the Holy Spirit.

The Work of the Spirit

For centuries, Christians have confessed their faith in God the Father Almighty, Maker of heaven and earth, and in Jesus Christ, God's only Son, our Lord. Concerning Jesus Christ, we affirm that He was conceived by the Holy Spirit and born of the virgin Mary.

Basic to this conviction of the work of the Spirit is the combined testimony of prophets and apostles. " . . . Behold," says Isaiah, "a virgin shall conceive, and bear a son, and shall call his name Immanuel" (7:14). Clearly, Isaiah "here refers to a remarkable miracle of God, and recommends it to the attentive and devout consideration of all the godly."[1] Seven centuries pass, and then the prophecy matures into history. Promise becomes fulfillment. By the work of the Holy Spirit, Jesus Christ comes into the world to save His people from their sins.

Matthew 1:18-25 tells us how the birth of Jesus Christ came about. Mary was pledged to be married to Joseph, but before they began to live together, she was found to be with child through the Holy Spirit. Joseph, being a righteous man, did not want to expose her to public disgrace but planned to divorce her quietly, until he learned the truth of the situation from an angel of the Lord. Then Joseph discovered that what was conceived in Mary was from the Holy Spirit. He agreed to take her home as his wife and to call the child *Jesus*. But he had no marital relationship with her until she gave birth to that unique son in fulfillment of Isaiah's ancient prophecy.

Luke 1:26-38 relates how God sent the angel Gabriel to the Galilean town of Nazareth. There God's messenger announced the most momentous news ever, to a virgin who was pledged to marry a carpenter. The angel told her that she had received grace from God and had been chosen to become the mother of Him who would be the Saviour of His people. This child would be great. Recognized as the Son of the Most High, there would be given to Him the throne of His ancestor David. His kingdom would be everlasting. When Mary, a virgin, wondered how this could happen, she was assured that the miraculous conception would be due to the power of the Holy Spirit. With obedient faith, Mary put herself at the Lord's disposal for the fulfillment of His saving purpose.

The immaculate conception of Jesus in the womb of the virgin Mary was the work of the Holy Spirit. The incarnation of the Son of God was not the result of Joseph's procreative power but of Jehovah's creative might. The Saviour was born without human paternity, dramatizing the fact that God so loved the world that He gave His unique Son to save sinners. Jesus Christ is the gift of God. " . . . Unto us a child is born, unto us a Son is given . . . " (Isa. 9:6). "Thanks be to God for his indescribable gift!" (II Cor. 9:15).

Undoubtedly, we are confronted here with "a divine miracle and a deep mystery, in which the work of the Holy Spirit must be glorified. . . . Wherefore let us look into this matter only with deepest reverence, and not advance theories contrary to the Word of God."[2] On the basis of Isaiah's prophecy and the New Testament evidence provided by Matthew and Luke, we ascribe to the Holy Spirit "the framing, forming, and miraculous conception of the body of Christ in the womb of the blessed Virgin."[3]

There are those who argue that the absence of this story in the writings of other prophets and apostles shows that either they didn't consider it important or didn't even accept it. These critics note that the virgin birth of Christ is not mentioned in the writings of Peter and Paul, and is apparently ignored by Mark and John. Therefore, they suggest, we need not insist on it today as a historical reality indispensable to Biblical faith.

Now it is true that Mark doesn't refer to this event. "But what of it?" asks a noted preacher. "Neither does he speak of the birth of Christ in any form whatever. Would you infer from that silence that therefore Jesus was never born, never came into the world at all? Certainly not. Where does Mark's gospel begin? With the baptism of Jesus, or the public life and ministry of Jesus. The fact that he does not write about the birth and childhood of Jesus in no way invalidates the facts related by Matthew and Luke. . . . You might as well argue that there was no Declaration of Independence and no Bunker Hill, because there is no mention of these events in a history of the United States which commenced with the Civil War."[4]

Does it really matter if the virgin birth of Christ is not mentioned in the Gospel of John? Neither is the transfiguration, nor the institution of the Lord's Supper. Are we to conclude, then, that they never took place? It is inadvisable to argue from silence in one gospel when there is abundant evidence in the others. How many times does God have to say something for it to be true? What is affirmed by Matthew and Luke is a sufficient basis for our belief in the virgin birth of Immanuel.

If the Bible cannot be trusted at this point, then can it be trusted when it relates Christ's compassionate ministry, incomparable parables, sacrificial death, and glorious resurrection? If it is not authentic and authoritative in these narratives, can it be regarded as consistently worthy of trust? "The Bible teaches the virgin birth of Christ; a man who accepts the virgin birth may continue to hold to the full truthfulness of the Bible; a man who rejects it cannot possibly do so. That much at least should be perfectly plain."[5]

The Spirit who wrought the miraculous conception of Jesus in the womb of the virgin Mary brings about our spiritual regeneration. He dispenses with human paternity and acts in sovereign grace to create new persons.

In discussing the encounter of men with Christ and describing their diverse responses to Him, the apostle John writes: "He was in the world, and though the world was made through him, the world did not recognize him. He came to that which was his own, but his own did not receive him. Yet to all who received him, to those who believed in his name, he gave the right to become children of God—children born not of natural descent, nor of human decision or a husband's will, but born of God" (John 1:10-13).

By a triple repudiation, the apostle denies that man's merit, intention, or power can gain him entrance into the family of God. "The natural and carnal means of blood, flesh, and the will of man, are rejected wholly in this matter, and the whole efficacy of the new birth is ascribed to God alone."[6] Beyond all question, "nothing human, however great or excellent, can bring about the birth of which John speaks."[7]

Some respond to Christ by ignoring, despising, or rejecting Him. Their refusal to receive Him betrays their unregenerate character and excludes them from participation in the life Christ brings. Those who are moved in the direction of this Lord and Saviour by the dynamic of faith show that they have indeed been "born of God." Their "faith is but the fruit of spiritual regeneration."[8]

In kindling and sustaining the flame of new life, God generally uses the Scriptures, especially the gospel. James affirms that God "chose to give us birth through the word of truth" (James 1:18). And Peter says that believers "have been born again, not of perishable seed, but of imperishable, through the living and enduring word of God" (I Peter 1:23).

Our regeneration, like the miraculous conception of Jesus in the womb of Mary, is God's work and not man's doing. In declaring that the children of God are born not of the will of man, nor of the will of the flesh, but of God, John "undoubtedly borrows this glorious description of our higher birth from the extraordinary act of God which scintillates in the conception and birth of Christ."[9] Indeed, "the process whereby those who receive Him become sons of God—are reborn or regenerate as sons of God—is as much due to the sole activity of God as was the birth into the world of Him who alone is in His right Son of God."[10]

Our rebirth is God's work, not man's. This is stressed by Jesus in His memorable dialogue with Nicodemus. "Flesh gives birth to flesh, but the Spirit gives birth to spirit" (John 3:6). Frail and fallible humanity generates only frail and fallible humanity. Human impulse or volition cannot produce members of the household of faith. Only the gracious power of the Holy Spirit can accomplish that. Regeneration is the result of the Spirit's work. We become new persons and share in God's family only because His lovingkindness causes us to experience "the washing of rebirth and renewal by the Holy Spirit" (Titus 3:5).

It is the Spirit who is the Lord and Giver of life. Our regeneration comes about not because of ritual observances, social improvements, or environmental changes, but only by His creative act of divine power on our personalities.

When the Spirit regenerates us, we receive eyes to perceive the reality of the kingdom of God. The Spirit gives us an "inward capacity or fitness for the kingdom of God . . . breaks the power of sin, and makes all things new."[11] It is the Spirit who deals with us in regenerating efficacy and conveys to us that everlasting life "whose secret and manifestation is love generated of the love of God. He ploughs the ground of the soul, convincing it of sin, righteousness, and judgment. He implants the vivifying seed, so that man is 'born again by the Word of God which liveth and abideth forever' (I Peter 1:23). He 'pours out the love of God in the heart' (Romans 5:5). He both gives the child-state and teaches the new-born child to understand it, to cry 'Abba, Father,' (Romans 8:15) to the Eternal and Invisible."[12]

The Wonder of Immanuel

After considering the work of the Spirit in Christ's virgin birth and our spiritual rebirth, we now consider the wonder of Immanuel. The unique person whose incarnation was wrought by the Holy Spirit is called"'Immanuel',—which means,'God with us'" (Matt. 1:23).

We believe that Jesus Christ is "God with us." We affirm His deity. This Wonderful Counselor, Father of Eternity, and Prince of Peace (Isa. 9:6) is also the Mighty God. Being "in very nature God," He possesses "equality with God" (Phil. 2:6). " . . . In Christ all the fulness of the Deity lives in bodily form" (Col. 2:9). Jesus Christ is God manifested in the flesh (I Tim. 3:16). Divine prerogatives belong to Him: the authority to forgive sins, raise the dead, and judge the world. Divine reverence is due to Him. It is the Father's will "that all may honor the Son just as they honor the Father. He who does not honor the Son does not honor the Father who sent him" (John 5:23).

Jesus Christ, Immanuel, is "God with us." As we confess His deity, we acknowledge His humanity. Without ceasing to be God's equal, He became as one of us through the miracle of the incarnation. This truth is especially stressed in the Letter to the Hebrews. There we learn that the Son of God "shared" in our "humanity so that by his death he might destroy him who holds the power of death—that is, the devil—and free those who all their lives were held in slavery by their fear of death" (2:14, 15). He came into this world, involved Himself in our predicament, in order to help us overcome iniquity and mortality. "For this reason he had to be made like his brothers in every way, in order that he might become a merciful and faithful high priest in service to God, and that he might make atonement for the sins of the people. Because he himself suffered when he was tempted, he is able to help those who are being tempted" (2:17, 18). We are encouraged by the reality of Immanuel. "For we do not have a high priest who is unable to sympathize with our weaknesses, but we have one who has been tempted in every way, just as we are—yet was without sin. Let us then approach the throne of grace with confidence, so that we may receive mercy and find grace to help us in our time of need" (4:15, 16).

The unique Person who was conceived by the Holy Spirit and born of the virgin Mary is Immanuel, "God with us," facing our trials and enduring our temptations. We can trust in His sympathy and understanding. But let us never forget that the purpose of His incarnation was redemptive. This Immanuel is also "Jesus," the one born to "save his people from their sins" (Matt. 1:21). His name is thus a mini-gospel, proclaiming the saving mission entrusted to Him by the Father. Christ came into the world to save His people from the penalty and power of their sins. The incarnation was for the redemption of God's elect, and in it we see the revelation of divine love. "This is how God showed his love among us: He sent his one and only Son into the world that we might live through him. This is love: not that we loved God, but that he loved us and sent his Son as an atoning sacrifice for our sins" (I John 4:9, 10). "We love because he first loved us" (I John 4:19).

---

1. John Calvin, *Commentary on a Harmony of the Evangelists, Matthew, Mark, and Luke*, trans. William Pringle, 3 vols. (Edinburgh: Calvin Translation Society, 1845-46), 1:104-5 (on Matt. 1:22).

2. Abraham Kuyper, *The Work of the Holy Spirit*, p. 81.

3. John Owen, *A Discourse Concerning the Holy Spirit*, p. 162.

4. Clarence Edward Macartney, *Twelve Great Questions About Christ* (New York: Revell, 1923), p. 22.

5. J. Gresham Machen, *The Virgin Birth of Christ*, 2d ed. (New York: Harper & Row, 1932), pp. 387f.

6. Owen, *Discourse Concerning the Holy Spirit*, p. 208.

7. Leon Morris, *The Gospel According to John*, The New International Commentary on the New Testament (Grand Rapids: Eerdmans, 1971), p. 101 (on John 1:13).

8. John Calvin, *Commentary on the Gospel According to John*, trans. William Pringle, 2 vols. (Edinburgh: Calvin Translation Society, 1847-60), 1:43 (on John 1:13).

9. Kuyper, *Work of the Holy Spirit*, p. 82.

10. William Temple, *Readings in St. John's Gospel* (London: Macmillan, 1945), p. 13.

11. George Smeaton, *The Doctrine of the Holy Spirit*, p. 71.

12. Handley C. G. Moule, *Veni Creator*, p. 74.

2

DESCENT OF THE DOVE

Matthew 3:13-17

"John the Baptist had been engaged in his strenuous ministry by the river Jordan for some weeks: no prophet had ever taken part in such a mighty spiritual awakening in the history of Israel. The whole nation had been stirred and shaken by the message of righteousness and repentance: the multitude of penitents who came to be baptized had no parallel in the life of Israel. People were in a state of deep expectation, looking for the One that should come; and John himself must have felt the suspense of that time of waiting for the expected Messiah."[1]

Then, suddenly, it happened. John the Baptist and Jesus of Nazareth met in a memorable encounter filled with significance for the ministry of John and the mission of Jesus. The relevance of what was seen and heard on that occasion reaches across the centuries to us today.

Recognition of Sinlessness

Recall Matthew's record of the event. It begins: "Then Jesus came from Galilee to the Jordan to be baptized by John. But John tried to deter him, saying, 'I need to be baptized by you, and do you come to me?' " (3:13, 14).

At first John declined to perform this baptism. He barred the way to the water, persisting in his refusal. Why did he shrink from the task? John recognized the sinlessness of Jesus. Others had come for the sign of cleansing, confessing their sins. But Jesus had no sin to confess, no repentance to make, no cleansing to receive. John perceived the moral glory of Jesus and thus refused to baptize Him as he had baptized others.

It was John who, by his own admission, needed to be baptized by Jesus. But Jesus was the Lord, and John was simply His servant—unworthy of carrying such a Master's sandals. Jesus was the Saviour, whose power would purge the souls of men by the inward ministry of His Spirit. Jesus was the Judge, who would sift and separate the wheat from the chaff in a final judgment decisive for the destinies of men. Was this Jesus now asking John for baptism? How could John honestly comply with the request of our Lord?

John recognized the sinlessness of Jesus. So did others in the gospels. Demons knew Him to be the Holy One of God. Pontius Pilate found no crime in Him. Pilate's wife was upset over the prospect that this innocent prisoner would be unjustly condemned. One of the two thieves crucified with Him acknowledged His innocence. After His death on the cross, a Roman centurion confessed that He was a righteous man. No one could convict Him of any sin. Here was the spotless Lamb of God. No wonder John refused to baptize Him!

Identification with Sinners

Jesus answered John's objection with tenderness and firmness. "Let it be so now; it is proper for us to do this to fulfill all righteousness" (Matt. 3:15). Only then did John yield and perform the baptism of our Lord.

John's initial surprise and hesitation implied that there was something strange in the request of Jesus. Now the Master's reply implied "that there was really some cause of wonder, and that what he now proposed was an exceptional, extraordinary act, and as such to be borne with and submitted."[2]

Even though Jesus had no sin to confess, no repentance to show, no cleansing to experience, yet it was fitting that both Jesus and John should proceed to the baptism. It was as necessary for Jesus to submit to the rite as for John to administer it. Why? Because "righteousness" had to be fulfilled; God's holy will required it.

The sinless Jesus came to save His people from their sins. To accomplish this salvation, it was necessary for Him to identify with sinners. Far more than eating and drinking with publicans and sinners would be involved in the redemptive task. Redemption meant identification with them, taking the cup of divine judgment filled by their sin, and bearing the penalty of their transgression personally.

Jesus "descended into the water burdened with our sins."[3] That is why John the Baptist declared Him to be "the Lamb of God, who takes away the sin of the world!" (John 1:29). The sins Jesus bore, He took upon Himself willingly and in our place, as our High Priest and Mediator.

The baptism of Jesus at the river Jordan was thus a prelude to that baptism of sacrificial suffering He would meet at the hill called Calvary. In baptism, Jesus publicly identified Himself with sinful humanity and dedicated His life to the redemption of His people. He made "a full and final commitment of all His powers to the task to which the Spirit of God had been leading."[4]

As Moses identified himself with a wayward people and offered himself as a substitute in their place to bear the divine displeasure they deserved (Exod. 32:31, 32), and as Paul expressed a similar wish with regard to an Israel estranged from God (Rom. 9:1-5), so Jesus presented Himself to the Father on behalf of others. But only the sinless Son of God could serve as substitute and sacrifice for sinners, and this He did with a costly, redemptive love.

In His baptism, the sinless Jesus stood where sinners stand.

On His cross, He died as they should have died. So complete was His identification with those He came to save that they could say: "But he was wounded for our transgressions, he was bruised for our iniquities; upon him was the chastisement that made us whole, and with his stripes we are healed. All we like sheep have gone astray; we have turned every one to his own way; and the Lord has laid on him the iniquity of us all" (Isa. 53:5, 6 RSV). "He himself bore our sins in his body on the cross, so that we might die to sins and live for righteousness" (I Peter 2:24).

Consecration for Service

When John baptized Jesus, something wonderful happened. " . . . At that moment heaven was opened, and he saw the Spirit of God descending on him like a dove" (Matt. 3:16).

Suddenly, "heaven was opened." This recalls several passages of Scripture. The prophet Isaiah once prayed, "O that thou wouldst rend the heavens and come down, that the mountains might quake at thy presence" (Isa. 64:1 RSV). And Ezekiel remembered, "In the thirtieth year, in the fourth month, on the fifth day of the month, as I was among the exiles by the river Chebar, the heavens were opened, and I saw visions of God" (Ezek. 1:1 RSV). Our Lord told Nathanael how he would someday "see heaven open, and the angels of God ascending and descending on the Son of Man" (John 1:51). Stephen, the young deacon martyred by the violence of malicious men, saw the glory of God, and Jesus exalted in heavenly majesty. He said, "Look, I see heaven open and the Son of Man standing at the right hand of God" (Acts 7:56). Now "in all these cases the essential idea suggested . . . is that of a renewed communication and extraordinary gifts from heaven to earth."[5] At the baptism of Jesus, too, God manifested His heavenly glory. The opening skies were a symbol of His divine presence.

The Spirit descended in the likeness of a dove. As the Spirit of God had brooded with loving concern over the face of the deep at the dawn of creation, so now the Spirit descended on Jesus as He was about to begin the work of re-creation among men. The gentleness and purity represented by the dove would be visible in the tenderness and compassion of Jesus Christ. Surely, "in this symbol has been held out to us an eminent token of sweetest consolation, that we may not fear to approach Christ, who meets us not in the formidable power of the Spirit but clothed with gentle and lovely grace."[6]

Scripture teaches that there are two natures in the one person of our Lord. As the eternal Son of God, He possesses all the fulness of the Godhead. As the child born of Mary, He needed the descent of the Spirit to endow Him for the work of salvation. This endowment had been promised in ancient times. Concerning the Messiah, it was written: "And the Spirit of the Lord shall rest upon him, the spirit of wisdom and understanding, the spirit of counsel and might, the spirit of knowledge and the fear of the Lord. And his delight shall be in the fear of the Lord. He shall not judge by what his eyes see, or decide by what his ears hear; but with righteousness he shall judge the poor, and decide with equity for the meek of the earth; and he shall smite the earth with the rod of his mouth, and with the breath of his lips he shall slay the wicked. Righteousness shall be the girdle of his waist, and faithfulness the girdle of his loins" (Isa. 11:2-5 RSV).

Luke's account of our Lord's baptism is followed by this significant comment: "Jesus, full of the Holy Spirit, returned from the Jordan and was led by the Spirit in the desert" (4:1). Evidently, the Spirit descended on Jesus "in some inscrutable specialty of presence and power."[7]

It is God's will that we should experience a similar fulness of the Spirit. Thus we are exhorted to "be filled with the Spirit" (Eph. 5:18). But what does the fulness of the Spirit mean? Is it synonymous with excitement, ecstasy, a "spiritual high," emotional upheaval, and a trip to the edge of irrationality?

Let us consider the New Testament evidence before coming to conclusions on the fulness of the Spirit. Filled with the Holy Spirit during Pentecost, believers intelligibly declared the wonders of God (Acts 2:4, 11); Peter confessed Christ courageously before an apostate hierarchy (Acts 4:8-12); the Jerusalem congregation proclaimed the Christian message with boldness in the face of persecution (Acts 4:31); Stephen saw the exalted Lord and prayed for his murderers (Acts 7:55, 59); Barnabas encouraged the new converts of Syrian Antioch to remain true to Christ despite the influence of a pagan environment (Acts 11:23); and Paul confronted Elymas on the island of Cyprus, exposing him as "a child of the devil and an enemy of everything that is right" (Acts 13:9, 10).

Over and over again, the fulness of the Spirit led these New Testament Christians to witness to Jesus Christ with faithfulness. When we are filled with the Spirit of Christ, we speak of our Lord and serve in His name. Considering the context in which Paul calls us to be filled with the Spirit, we see that the fulness of the Spirit has to do with evangelical and ethical realities in the relationships of daily living. If we are filled with the Spirit, we will "speak to one another" (Eph. 5:19). When we are harsh, critical, out of fellowship with other believers, we betray our spiritual emptiness rather than demonstrate the fulness of the Spirit. Again, if we are full of the Spirit, we will use "psalms, hymns, and spiritual songs" to "sing and make music" in our hearts (Eph. 5:19). The praise of God our Saviour is a sign of the plenitude of the Spirit (Eph. 5:18). So is the attitude of thanksgiving "to God the Father for everything, in the name of our Lord Jesus Christ" (Eph. 5:20).

Arrogance and pride fragment fellowship, whether in the church or in the family. But the fulness of the Spirit enables disciples to "submit to one another out of reverence for Christ" (Eph. 5:21). Such submission makes for a happy home. As wives submit, adjust, and accommodate to their husbands; as husbands submit to their wives after the pattern of Christ who loved the Church and gave Himself for its highest good; as children obey and honour their parents; as parents bring up their children in the ways of the Lord; all of these show signs of being

Spirit-filled and will be richly rewarded with the blessing of joy within their families (Eph. 5:22—6:4).

In the fulness of the Spirit, which for us is synonymous with surrender to the lordship of Jesus Christ, may we speak and serve to bring benefits to the lives of others and glory to God alone.

Proclamation of Sonship

While the descent of the Spirit brings power for service and witness, it also gives assurance of the Father's love. Recall the word spoken from heaven with impressive majesty. "This is my Son, whom I love; with him I am well-pleased" (Matt. 3:17).

The primary significance of the Spirit's descent is thus for assurance. "The power which is connected with the Spirit's descent is not so much an infusion of new energy as it is the assurance of a relationship, the relationship of sonship. . . . The first meaning of the descent of the Spirit as exposited by the heavenly message is sonship."[8]

Let us remember that Jesus is at the beginning of His ministry on earth. Though sinless, He has openly identified himself with sinners and submitted to a baptism which involves confession of sin and pleading for cleansing. He has committed Himself to the fulfillment of all righteousness. Christ will conform to the Father's will, no matter what the cost. Although He is God's equal, yet He has also become man and taken on the role of a servant. In this humbling, painful service, He must persevere faithfully even to the extent of sacrifice. Because of His willingness to be "obedient to death—even death on a cross " (Phil. 2:8), the Father loves Him. Some day, the Father shall crown the perfection of the Son's obedience with supreme lordship and everlasting glory. But for now, Jesus must go on to Galilee, Gethsemane, and Golgotha. He moves in the full assurance of His Father's love.

The apostle Paul develops this truth of the Spirit's presence as assurance of sonship in his letters to the churches of Rome and Galatia. The Father, says Paul, assures us of our membership in His family through the indwelling of the Holy Spirit.

Writing to the Galatians, the apostle notes that God's children belong to "the family of believers" (6:10; 3:7). Because they have the openness of "faith," they "receive the promise of the Spirit" (3:14). All this is related to the person and work of Jesus Christ. For "when the time had fully come, God sent his Son, born of a woman, born under law, to redeem those under law, that we might receive the full rights of sons" (4:4-5). The reassuring truth is that God has "sent the Spirit of his Son into our hearts, the Spirit who calls out, 'Abba, Father!' " (4:6).

In his correspondence to the Christian community at Rome, Paul comments: "Those who are led by the Spirit of God are sons of God. For you did not receive a spirit that makes you a slave again to fear, but you received the Spirit who makes you sons. And by him we cry, 'Abba, Father.' The Spirit himself testifies with our spirit that we are God's children. Now if we are children, then we are heirs—heirs of God and co-heirs with Christ, if indeed we share in his sufferings in order that we may share in his glory" (8:14-17).

The descent of the dove and the voice from heaven not only bring an assurance of sonship, they also remind us what our redemption cost the God of glory. To save sinners, He did not send an angel, nor a mere man, but His own beloved Son. "He who did not spare his own Son, but gave him up for us all . . ." (Rom. 8:32). "This is how God showed his love among us: He sent his one and only Son into the world that we might live through him. This is love: not that we loved God, but that he loved us and sent his Son as an atoning sacrifice for our sins" (I John 4:9, 10). "For God so loved the world that he gave his one and only Son, that whoever believes in him shall not perish but have everlasting life" (John 3:16).

---

1. Marcus Loane, *The Keswick Week 1968* (London: Marshall, Morgan & Scott), p. 45.

2. Joseph Addison Alexander, *The Gospel According to Matthew* (New York: Scribner, 1867), p. 70 (on Matt. 3:15).

3. Abraham Kuyper, *The Work of the Holy Spirit*, p. 98.

4. W. W. Bryden, *The Spirit of Jesus in St. Paul*, p. 219.

5. Alexander, *Gospel According to Matthew*, p. 72 (on Matt. 3:16).

6. John Calvin, *Commentary on a Harmony of the Evangelists, Matthew, Mark, and Luke*, trans. William Pringle, 3 vols. (Edinburgh: Calvin Translation Society, 1845-46), 1:204 (on Matt. 3:16).

7. Handley C. G. Moule, *Veni Creator*, p. 32.

8. Frederick Dale Bruner, *A Theology of the Holy Spirit*, pp. 226f.

3

ENCOUNTER IN THE
WILDERNESS

Matthew 4:1-11

Have you ever reviewed the geography of the life of Jesus?
Think of His baptism at the river Jordan, the Sermon on the
Mount, His walking on the water of the sea, and the meeting in
the highlands of Galilee following the resurrection. His encounter with Satan in the wilderness also has great significance.
From that temptation of our Lord, we may learn lessons of lasting
worth.

The Spirit

The synoptic gospels all tell the story of the temptation of
Jesus, and all refer to the role of the Spirit in that encounter with
the evil one. Matthew mentions that after His baptism, Jesus was
led by the Spirit into a desert to be tempted by the devil (4:1).
Luke records the very same (4:1). Mark puts the matter even
more strongly. He remarks that the Spirit sent Jesus out into the
desert, driving Him powerfully to that confrontation with the
adversary (1:12).

Surely, we should not conclude from this that the Spirit had some sinister purpose in exposing Jesus to the attacks of the prince of darkness. Nor should we suppose that the Messiah had to be compelled by the Spirit, against His own will, to face the foe in that fierce struggle. The temptation occurred soon after the baptism at the Jordan. The descent of the dove and the voice from heaven were followed by the appearance of Satan and the voice of the tempter. Jesus went to that place of conflict in the desert, aware of the Spirit's leading, encouragement, and strength. He moved forward with high resolve to inflict a crushing defeat on the devil at the very outset of His messianic career.

By the Spirit Jesus was "guided, directed, comforted, supported, in the whole course of His ministry, temptation, obedience, and sufferings."[1] In the desert, therefore, we see Jesus "tempering His steel in the fire of the infernal adversary's dialectic"[2] at the prompting of the Spirit. Thus He moved forward to conflict and victory under the direction of the Holy Spirit.

The New Testament affirms that Old Testament prophets knew the direction of the Holy Spirit. The revelations they brought originated not in any human impulse but from the very heart and mind of God. They were led, carried along, borne aloft, by the wind of the Spirit in the process of prophesying (II Peter 1:21).

Likewise, we are told that Philip the evangelist was guided by the Holy Spirit from one place of service and witness to another. After he had evangelized the treasurer of the Ethiopian queen by pointing him to Christ crucified as the Saviour worthy of personal trust, Philip was led by the Spirit to go and preach the gospel to people in other regions as well (Acts 8:39, 40).

What does it mean for us to be led by the Spirit? In the eighth chapter of his Letter to the Romans, the apostle Paul declares that the members of God's family are known by the fact that they are led by the Spirit of God (8:14). But what does it mean to be led by the Spirit?

At this point, we must recognize and reject an unhealthy,

unscriptural subjectivism which considers its own preferences and prejudices as "the leading of the Spirit." Such rationalization often tries to justify what can never be sanctified. It is a camouflage to cover an operation whereby one's egoism seeks gratification!

If we are to understand what it means to be led by the Spirit, we must remember who the Spirit of Christ really is. Then we will have a clearer idea as to where He would lead us. For example, we are told in the Bible that He is the Spirit of truth (John 14:16; 16:13). His purpose is to guide us into an understanding of the gospel truth which centers in Jesus Christ. He does not give us new revelations, as some fanatical groups claim today, but enlightens our minds to understand what is already revealed in the inspired Scriptures of the Old and New Testaments. To be led by the Spirit is to appreciate and accept the message of God's Word.

Again, He is the Spirit of grace and supplication (Zech. 12:10). He leads us to Calvary, so that we may look on Him whom we have pierced and mourn because of Him. The Spirit leads us to heartbroken repentance. He is the Spirit of faith, directing us to move toward Jesus for salvation (II Cor. 4:13). As four friends brought the paralytic to Jesus for wholeness, so the Spirit brings us to the Saviour as He creates and sustains faith in Christ.

He is the Spirit of holiness (Rom. 1:4). He leads us to die unto sin and live unto righteousness, so that our growth in holiness is furthered. Any attitude or action that feeds the old nature and starves the new cannot ever be ascribed to the leading of the Holy Spirit. He is the Spirit of glory (I Peter 4:14). His ministry is to glorify Christ, our Lord and Saviour. He inspires the song of glory, the doxology of the redeemed heart grateful for the wonders of God's grace. And at the last, He will lead the suffering saints through exhausting toils and fiery trials to the glorious Canaan of heavenly glory and everlasting blessedness.

Is the leading of the Spirit of Christ, who speaks in Holy Scripture, a reality in our lives?

The Seducer

Biblical revelation is utterly realistic. It does not ignore or hide the existence of the evil one, but exposes the enemy of God and man. He is indicated and indicted as the adversary who constantly contradicts the Creator, seeks to disorder the creation, and is determined to bring about the destruction of God's creatures. The devil is a roaring lion, a crafty serpent, a dreadful dragon. This grim prince of darkness sometimes masquerades as an angel of light to deceive and destroy the unwary. His malignant shadow is over the world. He holds it in his grip. He is the father of lies, misrepresenting God to man and men to God. The devil blinds the eyes of men to their true spiritual predicament as sinners and keeps from them the blessings of the gospel of Christ. Above all, he desperately tries to prevent men from perceiving the glory of the Lord Jesus and turning to Christ alone for salvation (II Cor. 4:4).

There has been a morbid preoccupation with satanism and the occult at times, but for the most part people go to the other extreme of questioning and denying the existence of Satan. This suits him and promotes his purposes, for "Satan has very little trouble with those who do not believe in him; they are already on his side."[3]

However, Scripture does speak of the devil. In view of this fact, one may take either of several positions on the matter. Either Christ and the apostles were accommodating their language to a gross superstition and knew it to be such (in which case they would be guilty of deceit); or they shared in this superstition, not knowing it to be such (in which case they would be demonstrating ignorance); or they taught the actual truth regarding the existence of the devil (in which case we must reckon with him realistically).

The gospels present the story of Jesus' temptation as a historical event, not as myth or allegory. The seducer of souls actually dared to attack the Son of God in that wilderness encounter. He had the audacity to mount an assault against the Messiah. This he did in three ways during those forty days.

First, he suggested that the hungry Jesus turn stones into bread. Plausible enough. Why not ease the pangs of hunger for Yourself and others? This will fulfill popular expectations and advance Your own cause. Why not turn stones into bread? We have here the impetus of "the reasonableness of materialism pounding at the gates of the spiritual citadel."[4]

Next, came a temptation to create faith and loyalty by the use of the extraordinary and the exceptional. Leap from the temple pinnacle, and let that spectacular action recruit a following for Your cause. Dazzle the people with someting sensational, and they'll acclaim You as their hero. Go ahead. God will take care of You. Leap!

Finally, Satan suggested that all the powers of this world would be given to Jesus on one condition: that He change His loyalty from the Father of glory to the father of lies. "All this will I give you," said Satan, "if you will bow down and worship me" (Matt. 4:9).

The same spiritual adversary who tempted Jesus then, tempts us now. Sometimes, he uses persecution. He goes about as a roaring lion, furiously and fiercely in search of prey. He is determined to destroy and devour. He tempts through intimidation. In the course of history, Satan has used the fear of physical danger, the violence that imprisons, tortures, and murders. Under such assaults, men have been known to "break" and recant. The devil also uses the fear of social ostracism. Who wants to risk ridicule as an obscurantist for holding to the historic Christian faith, or be considered puritannical for insisting on the abiding authority and relevance of God's Word for human behavior? Again, Satan uses the fear of economic reprisal as a weapon of temptation. It is one thing to sing from "A Mighty Fortress Is Our God":

> Let goods and kindred go, this mortal life also;
> The body they may kill: God's truth abideth still,
> His kingdom is for ever.

It is quite another thing, however, to give up an academic post, a prestigious pulpit, splendid property, or a comfortable pension in order to remain loyal to the Lord after all efforts at reformation from within have proven fruitless.

What Satan does not accomplish through pressures, he tries to achieve by false but alluring promises. The roaring lion leaves the scene and returns as an angel of light. His tactic is deception here. It is obvious that the devil deceives people into imagining that rebellion against parental authority, perversion of sexuality through sensuality and immorality, misappropriation of money and property, lying, and voracious greed are somehow "good" for us and are exempt from judgment. What is not so evident, however, is the fact that the devil tries to deceive disciples and denominations with his false promises. For example, he whispers that "narrow-minded" insistence on the historic Christian faith and spiritual discipline will only alienate people. If you want to gain more members and increase your influence in the community, the smart thing to do is accommodate to the rationalism and new morality of the present situation. Such "relevance" is bound to make your impact much more significant on society!

Or, the devil will try to tell you that the smart thing to do is amalgamate the gospel with some social, political, or economic theory in order to give it more popular appeal. Yesterday called for the admixture of nationalism or capitalism. Today may call for the additive of socialism or communism. Tomorrow, it could be nihilism or some other *ism*. But don't ever proclaim the unadulterated gospel in all its Scriptural simplicity if you want to reach your generation!

Again, Satan often suggests that we isolate the elements of

Biblical faith, so as to exaggerate some and neglect others. Stress creedal orthodoxy, insist on a confessional position true to the Word, but in the process let go of brotherly love so that the first casualty in any controversy is the community Christ came to create. Or, put such a premium on fellowship that truth is relegated to the periphery if it poses a threat to organizational unity.

The devil deceives ministers of the gospel into pride of achievement or jealousy over someone else's accomplishment. He lures them into busyness and the wilderness of confused priorities, so that they spend too much time "running around" and too little in disciplined study; or he keeps them hidden in the study to escape contact with the people who need pastoral care. Above all, he tempts them to neglect the family, the primary parish, on the pretext that they must get on with "the Lord's work." I know from personal experience: Satan's most vulnerable target in the ministry is the "workaholic" who has delusions of omnicompetence and even omnipotence despite formal professions of faith and prayers of dependence. Surely, we must recognize these satanic suggestions for what they are!

Let us be aware of the fact that Satan tempts men "to believe that there are more real factors in life than the unobtrusive presence and power of God; that, moreover, there is a higher virtue on earth than the courage to trust that power; that above all, there is something more wonderful in life than just ordinary life lived according to the Will of God."[5]

The Scripture

It is certainly most remarkable that in the wilderness encounter, both Jesus and Satan made reference to what was written in the Old Testament. From what they said, and the way they said it, we may learn some vital lessons about the use and abuse of Holy Scripture.

Consider, for example, the way Satan abused God's written Word to encourage an act of presumption. He quoted the promise of divine protection in Psalm 91:11, 12 out of its context in order to get Jesus to leap from the temple pinnacle (Matt. 4:6). Satan still distorts the real meaning of Scripture, so that men will sin to their own loss.

Consider the familiar passage in II Corinthians 3:6 concerning the letter killing but the Spirit giving life. Satan would have men abuse that passage to yield the following unwarranted meaning: It is deadening to take the Bible literally; it is the spirit of the thing that counts. But the apostle is saying nothing of the sort. He is declaring that the letter of God's law accuses us and sentences us to death on account of our transgressions, but that the Holy Spirit brings us life through the forgiveness of sins and release from condemnation in the gospel.

Again, some Scripture regarding freedom in Christ (such as John 8:32 and Galatians 5:1) has been abused to justify homosexual practices. At a recent gathering, a bevy of "gay" clerics told the other clergy assembled there that what they were doing was not at all contrary to nature, as "narrow-minded" Paul insisted, but merely opposed to custom, which is subject to change. In their thinking, what they were doing was simply a variant lifestyle and an authentic expression of their freedom in Christ from traditional restrictions.

There is also frequent abuse of those texts which speak of the spiritual unity of the Father and the Son and the regenerate community of faith with the Father and the Son. So, John 17:18-23 is made to support ecclesiastical mergers without regard to sound doctrine. Thus an indiscriminate ecumenism seeks to validate the creation of amorphous conglomerates or the formation of larger pressure groups for the promotion of a secularized gospel.

All who abuse the written Word in this way commit a grave error. We must ever be on guard "against being led by a false application of Scripture into the snares of Satan."[6] The right use of Scripture involves considering a text in its context, with reverent regard for its divine authority and humble dependence on the Spirit, who inspired it, for enlightenment.

Our Lord clearly considers the Old Testament writings to

possess indisputable authority. Scripture has come through men, but from God. The Bible has authority because of its ultimate Author. Thus Jesus makes His appeal to what is written. He lays hold of the sword of the Spirit, the Word of God, in the combat against Satan.

He refuses to turn stones into bread because "It is written: 'Man does not live on bread alone, but on every word that comes from the mouth of God' " (Matt. 4:4; Deut. 8:3).

The Scripture quoted by our Lord, remarks Calvin, "condemns the stupidity of those who reckon life to consist in luxury and abundance; while it reproves the distrust and inordinate anxiety which drives us to seek unlawful means. The precise object of Christ's reply is this: We ought to trust in God for food, and for other necessities of the present life, in such a manner that none may overleap the barriers which God has prescribed. But if Christ did not consider himself at liberty to change stones into bread, without the command of God, much less is it lawful for us to procure food by fraud, or robbery, or violence, or murder."[7]

Surely, Jesus is not indifferent to the cry for bread. He blesses loaves and fishes and feeds the hungry thousands. But He is convinced that the primary hunger of the human heart is for the Word of the living God. "The vision of social amelioration without spiritual regeneration has constituted a temptation to which many important men in history have succumbed completely." Jesus doesn't deny "that men must be fed, or that social justice must be preached; but He asserts that these things are not first."[8] Beware of the peril of making men richer without making them holier.

Jesus would not leap from the temple pinnacle because "It is also written: 'Do not put the Lord your God to the test' " (Matt. 4:7; Deut. 6:16). Do not presume on God's power, putting Him to the test by thoughtless, reckless action. We are not justified in risking our lives arbitrarily and then expecting God to send His angels to protect us.

A sensational, spectacular leap by Jesus might have given momentary stimulation to the jaded, bored spirits of the populace, but it would have done nothing to change their hearts. And it "would not have been an act of trust in God at all: it would have been flinging a challenge in God's face and forcing God's hand. Jesus would not have anything to do with that."[9]

Nor would Jesus switch His allegiance from the Lord God to Satan in order to gain all the kingdoms of the world and their splendor, because it is written, "Worship the Lord your God, and serve him only" (Matt. 4:10; Deut. 6:13). The refusal of Jesus is vigorous and vehement. He makes His appeal once more to Scripture. "What is written gives to Him the final, conclusive answer."[10]

The disciple of Jesus will want to share the Master's high view of the written Word. Willingly he submits himself to the authority of Scripture. This means more than buying a Bible, reading it occasionally, hearing it faithfully preached, or even defending it as God's inspired Word. It means believing the Word, treasuring it in our hearts, obeying it in our lives.

If what is written in the Bible is also inscribed at the control center of our being, then we will make the right response when tempted by the devil. The truth of God will be brought to mind by the Spirit who inspired the Scriptures, countering every satanic suggestion.

The devil may say, "Get all you can, no matter how. Honesty is not the best policy. If you don't look after yourself, nobody will. And, besides, everybody's doing it." The believer will respond from Exodus 20:15-17, "It is written: 'Thou shalt not steal. Thou shalt not bear false witness. . . . Thou shalt not covet."

Satan may suggest, "What's wrong with having an affair? Some new relationship and stimulating sexual involvement may actually save your fading marriage. Go ahead. Let it happen. Your private life is no one's business but your own." But the Christian in whose heart God's Word is decisive will reply, "It is written, 'Thou shalt not commit adultery' " (Exod. 20:14).

The adversary may insinuate that church fellowship should be restricted to people who are "of our kind," and suggest that others would really feel happier among their own ethnic, racial, or social group. But the man who is subject to the Word of God will resist the temptation of divisive prejudices, saying, "It is written, 'There is neither Jew nor Greek, slave nor free, male nor female, for you are all one in Christ Jesus' " (Gal. 3:28).

The New Testament saint, like the Old Testament psalmist, says: "With my whole heart have I sought thee: O let me not wander from thy commandments. Thy word have I hid in mine heart, that I might not sin against thee" (Ps. 119:10, 11).

The Saviour

Jesus was "no sooner out of the water of baptism, but in the fire of temptation."[11] But He resolutely rejected all that was opposed to God's will. He triumphed over the tempter. Thrusting aside the false standards suggested by Satan, Jesus revealed life's true standard—humble, faithful, costly obedience to the will of the Father.

From Jesus, who experienced temptation, we may receive sympathy. He knows what it means to face the whole empire of evil and engage the prince of darkness in fierce combat. He encountered and resisted the pressures and promises of Satan. Susceptible to the temptations that beset us, the incarnate Son of God endured the full force of those temptations. Now He can sympathize with us when our spirit may be willing but our weak flesh is attracted by temptation. This sympathy of Jesus "with the sinner in his trial does not depend on the experience of sin, but on the experience of the strength of the temptation to sin, which only the sinless can know in its fullest intensity. He who falls yields before the last strain."[12] Jesus, therefore, understands the temptations we encounter. Turning to Him, we discover a Friend who knows and cares.

If, when tempted, we yield—what then? The apostle John deals with this problem when he writes words which shatter the presumption of the self-righteous even as they deliver the penitent from despair. He declares: "My dear children, I write this to you so that you will not sin. But if anybody does sin, we have one who speaks to the Father in our defense—Jesus Christ, the Righteous One. He is the atoning sacrifice for our sins, and not only for ours but also for the sins of the whole world" (I John 2:1, 2). "If we confess our sins, he is faithful and just and will forgive us our sins and purify us from all unrighteousness" (I John 1:9).

Let no one imagine himself to be immune from the attacks of Satan. Such pride leads to a lack of prayerfulness and vigilance, opening the way for the tempter to do his deadly work. Let us never forget that "the tempter is restless and impudent; so that a man is to expect, if he live out his days, to be urged to all sins, to the breach of every branch of the ten commandments, and to be put to it in respect of every article of the Creed."[13]

James, the servant of our Lord advises: "Submit yourselves, then, to God. Resist the devil, and he will flee from you" (4:7). And the apostle Peter, who was once ambushed by the evil one because of his failure to be on the alert and continue in an attitude of prayer, now warns us: "Your enemy the devil prowls around like a roaring lion looking for someone to devour. Resist him, standing firm in the faith" (I Peter 5:8, 9).

We can resist the evil one and overcome every temptation to distrust or disobey as we draw upon the boundless resources of God offered us in the gospel. When the Word of Christ gives us a clear sense of direction, and when the Spirit of Christ provides us with the powerful dynamic we need, victory is ours. We are more than conquerors through Him who loves us!

———————

1. John Owen, *A Discourse Concerning the Holy Spirit*, p. 174.

2. Henri Daniel-Rops, *Jesus and His Times*, trans. Ruby Millar (New York: Dutton, 1954), p. 188.

3. Fulton J. Sheen, *Life of Christ* (New York: McGraw-Hill, 1958), p. 60.

4. W. W. Bryden, *The Spirit of Jesus in St. Paul*, p. 227.

5. Ibid., p. 231.

6. John Calvin, *Commentary on a Harmony of the Evangelists, Matthew, Mark, and Luke*, trans. William Pringle, 3 vols. (Edinburgh: Calvin Translation Society, 1845-46), 1:218 (on Matt. 4:6).

7. Ibid., p. 215 (on Matt. 4:4).

8. Sheen, *Life of Christ*, pp. 61ff.

9. James S. Stewart, *The Life and Teaching of Jesus Christ* (Edinburgh: Church of Scotland Committee on Publications, 1954), p. 49.

10. Norval Geldenhuys, *Commentary on the Gospel of Luke*, The New International Commentary on the New Testament (Grand Rapids: Eerdmans, 1952), p. 161 (on Luke 4:8).

11. John Trapp, *A Commentary on the Old and New Testaments*, ed. Hugh Martin, 5 vols. (London: Dickinson, 1867-77), 5:25 (on Matt. 4:1).

12. Brooke Foss Westcott, *The Epistle to the Hebrews*, 3d ed. (London: Macmillan, 1914), pp. 59-60 (on Heb. 2:18).

13. Trapp, *Old and New Testaments*, 5:314 (on Luke 4:13).

4

THE LORD'S ANOINTED

Luke 4:13-28

After encountering, resisting, and overcoming the devil in the wilderness, Jesus returned to Galilee in the power of the Spirit. News about Him spread throughout the countryside. He taught in the synagogues and met with great acceptance. On one memorable occasion, He went to Nazareth (His childhood home). On the Sabbath day He was in the local synagogue. As the worship service progressed, Jesus participated by reading from the book of the prophet Isaiah (Isa. 61:1, 2). Then He rolled up the sacred scroll, gave it back to the attendant, and sat down. As He prepared to expound on the prophecy, the eyes of everyone in the synagogue fastened on Him. What would He say? We know now what He said. "Today this scripture is fulfilled in your hearing" (Luke 4:21).

As we consider this text, we are confronted with the messianic consciousness of Jesus. His consciousness should help us to become aware of our privileges and obligations as members of the messianic community.

Messianic Consciousness

Jesus said, "The Spirit of the Lord is on me" (Luke 4:18). To

Him the Spirit was given without measure (John 3:34). The Spirit, descending on Him at the baptism and abiding with Him through the wilderness temptation, endowed His human nature "with glorious gifts, powers, and faculties."[1] These became operative in the course of His ministry and enabled Him to fulfill His mission. The Spirit empowered Him, not for personal enjoyment, but for redemptive service.

Jesus refers to Himself as "anointed" with "the Spirit of the Lord" (Luke 4:18). Old Testament prophets, priests, and kings were solemnly set apart to their respective offices through an act of anointing, symbolic of endowment with grace from above for service on earth (I Kings 19:16; Lev. 8:12). Jesus now declares Himself to be the Lord's "anointed," the Messiah or Christ of God, endowed with the Holy Spirit beyond measure, to serve as the Prophet, Priest, and King of His people.

While many did not recognize Jesus as the Messiah in the days of His flesh, Simon Peter was given an insight by the heavenly Father into the true nature of His person and work. At Caesarea Philippi, enlightened of God, Peter recognized and confessed Jesus to be "the Christ, the Son of the living God" (Matt. 16:16). This recognition of Jesus as "Christ," or *Messiah,* is basic to the Church's security. So long as we believe in Him as the Lord's anointed and receive Him as our infallible Prophet, merciful Priest, and only King, the gates of hell shall not prevail against us.

Jesus is anointed by the Spirit "to preach good news to the poor" (Luke 4:18). When John the Baptist experienced spiritual depression in the fortress dungeon of Macherus, he wondered if Jesus was really the Messiah. Anxious for reassurance, he sent messengers to Jesus, asking, "Are you the one who was to come, or should we expect someone else?" Jesus replied, "Go back and report to John what you hear and see: The blind receive sight, the lame walk, those who have leprosy are cured, the deaf hear, the dead are raised, and the good news is preached to the poor" (Matt. 11:3-5).

One of the main features of the messianic community is this:

the evangelization of the poor. What kind of poor? We must be concerned over the root causes of human poverty in the world. We dare not be indifferent to economic injustice. "The truly pious man is emphatically not one who, though scrupulous with regard to all the formal observances of religion, neglects the requirements of mercy."[2]

But while we need our daily bread to live, we do not live by bread alone. Spiritual poverty, marked by lack of pardon, peace, and power is "the condition of all of us without Christ."[3] This poverty can only be remedied by reaching out with faith's empty hands to receive the riches of Christ. "Blessed are the poor in spirit, for theirs is the kingdom of heaven" (Matt. 5:3).

The Messiah is also "sent . . . to proclaim freedom for the prisoners" (Luke 4:18). He knows Himself to be sent into this world by the Father on a mission. Jesus Christ has an apostolate to fulfill. A clear sense of purpose shapes His thought and action. This mission involves the proclamation of freedom for the prisoners. In what sense should we understand this liberating aspect of the Messiah's ministry?

Those who advocate the utter secularization of the gospel and interpret salvation as the attainment of leftist utopias, sanction not only civil disobedience but also destructive terrorism and armed rebellion in Christ's name. Some have even gone to the extreme of asserting that God has sanctified violence into an instrument of redemption. Their misunderstanding of the Biblical evangel has led them to substitute revolution and anarchy for redemption and freedom. They have traded away the birthright of the glorious liberty of God's children for a Marxist mess of pottage.

God alone is Lord of the conscience. Whenever the demands of civil government conflict with God's, believers must obey God rather than men. They will render to Caesar the things that are Caesar's, but never the things that are God's. We will resist human tyranny in pursuit of freedom under law out of a higher loyalty to the Lord alone.

The freedom Christ proclaims, according to the Scriptures, is a freedom from the penalty and the power of sin. He liberates men from the penalty of sin by taking the condemnation of sinners on Himself and suffering in His own body the judgment deserved by their sins. Christ delivers from doom all who trust in Him as their Saviour. He sets us free from the curse of the divine law we had broken, "by becoming a curse for us" (Gal. 3:13).

Our Lord also liberates men from the power of sin. Somerset Maugham may write *Of Human Bondage* and Luther *The Bondage Of The Will,* but we know from personal experience that habitual yielding to sin is spiritual slavery. We also know the truth if we believe in the Christ of the gospel and surrender our lives to Him. In such commitment is real freedom. Jesus says, "Everyone who sins is a slave to sin. . . . If the Son sets you free, you will be free indeed" (John 8:34, 36).

Jesus has been anointed and sent "to proclaim . . . recovery of sight for the blind" (Luke 4:18). In His merciful works of healing, He has manifested His compassionate concern for the sightless. The example of Christ is still the inspiration for medical missions today. But we must look beyond the cure of physical blindness to see the deeper significance of these words. The sad fact is that "the god of this age has blinded the minds of unbelievers, so that they cannot see the light of the gospel of the glory of Christ, who is the image of God" (II Cor. 4:4). The grim reality is that "the man without the Spirit does not accept the things that come from the Spirit of God, for they are foolishness to him, and he cannot understand them, because they are spiritually discerned" (I Cor. 2:14). But when God touches us in His sovereign grace and our souls receive the healing touch of the Saviour, we perceive "the light of the knowledge of the glory of God in the face of Christ" (II Cor. 4:6).

Messiah comes "to release the oppressed" (Luke 4:18). For He is the anointed of God, anointed with the Spirit and sent into the world. He comes to release the oppressed. Do we feel the pressure of anxiety, the load of guilt, the crush of anguish, the weight of failure, the burden of dread? Christ comes "to comfort and cure afflicted consciences, to give peace to those that are troubled and humbled for sins, and under a dread of God's wrath against them, and to bring them to rest who are weary and heavy laden."[4]

In Christ, God draws near "to rescue us from the deep abyss of death, to restore us to complete happiness. . . . We cannot enjoy those benefits which Christ bestows, in any other manner, than by being humbled under a deep conviction of our distresses, and by coming as hungry souls, to seek him as our deliverer: for all who swell with pride, and do not groan under their captivity, nor are displeased with their blindness, lend a deaf ear" to this prophetic promise, and "treat it with contempt."[5]

It is the mission of the Messiah "to proclaim the year of the Lord's favor" (Luke 4:19). In the Old Testament, liberty was proclaimed to all the inhabitants of the land of Israel in the year of jubilee (Lev. 25:8-17). With the sounding of the trumpet, debts were forgiven, slaves released, and lost inheritances restored to their original owners. The coming of Jesus brings in "the age of the Messiah, which is Jehovah's great time for bestowing great blessings on His people."   The reference is, therefore, not to an ordinary year, but the whole period of salvation which God inaugurates with the appearance of the Messiah.   ". . . Now is the time of God's favor, now is the day of salvation" (II Cor. 6:2).

Messianic Community

Jesus was aware of being anointed with the Spirit and conscious of His calling as the Christ of God. How did the people in that synagogue at Nazareth react to His interpretation of Isaiah's prophetic promise regarding the Messiah? After Jesus announced the fulfillment of the Scripture in Himself, some responded with wonder. They were "amazed at the gracious words that came from his lips" (Luke 4:22). But soon their admiration and enthusiasm gave way to doubt. How could "Joseph's son" make such astounding claims for Himself? The people made Jesus feel the pain of rejection, so that He exclaimed, "No prophet is accepted in his home town" (Luke 4:24). Jesus referred to the fact that Elijah and Elisha found greater acceptance among outsiders like Sidonians and Syrians than among their own kinsmen in Israel. When the people heard this, they were furious. "They got up, drove him out of the town, and took him to the brow of the hill on which the town was built, in order to throw him down the cliff" (Luke 4:29). They reacted with "rationalizing doubt, offence, rejection, wrath, and murderous hatred."[8] But Jesus "walked right through the crowd and went on his way" (Luke 4:30).

Does the story end with the majestic departure of Jesus from the town whose people rejected Him as the Christ? And can we merely look at that event as spectators? Not at all. The Jesus who was anointed with the Holy Spirit and declared Himself to be the Messiah calls us to be a messianic community of prophets, priests, and kings. He anointed us with the same Spirit and sends us forth with a mission to fulfill.

The apostle John refers to this anointing of believers in a most interesting context. He calls attention to the fact that "this is the last hour" of world history. We have entered the final phase before the Lord's return. The Antichrist is about to appear, but already "many antichrists have come." They do not belong to the fellowship of the true Church, and have indeed departed from its standards of faith and life (I John 2:18, 19). "But you," affirms the apostle, "have an anointing from the Holy One, and all of you know the truth" (I John 2:20). Unlike those who are teachers of lies, they do not deny but rather confess "that Jesus is the Christ" (I John 2:22). Religious liars and apostates may try to lead them astray. But "the anointing you received from him remains in you, and you do not need anyone to teach you. But as his anointing teaches you about all things and as that anointing is real, not counterfeit—just as it has taught you, remain in him" (I John 2:27).

What does this mean to us? We may say what it does not mean, first of all. It does not mean that every Christian knows everything there is to know and can dispense with the teaching ministry expressly appointed by Christ for the benefit of His people

(Matt. 28:19; Eph. 4:11). On the positive side, what John is saying is that believers are anointed with the Holy Spirit and thus enlightened concerning the great, central truths of the gospel. They have an insight into the person and work of Jesus the Messiah. Such is the renewing influence of the Holy Spirit on our minds that "we come to see and discern spiritual things in a spiritual manner." Thus we "savingly know God and his mind as revealed in and by Jesus Christ."[9] That is why Paul writes to the Ephesians: "I keep asking that the God of our Lord Jesus Christ, the glorious Father, may give you the Spirit of wisdom and revelation, so that you may know him better. I pray also that the eyes of your heart may be enlightened" (1:17, 18).

If John writes of our anointing, and Paul prays for our enlightenment, it is Peter who reminds us of our function as members of the messianic community. We have a service to render. And what is it? To be "a chosen people, a royal priesthood, a holy nation, a people belonging to God." Why? "That you may declare the praises of him who called you out of darkness into his wonderful light" (I Peter 2:9). We are anointed to fulfill a prophetic, priestly, and regal function in this world to the glory of God our Saviour.

The Heidelberg Catechism of 1563 sets forth the close connection between Christ and Christians when it asks and answers these important questions:

> "Q. 31. Why is he called *Christ,* that is, the *Anointed* One?
> A.   Because he is ordained of God the Father, and anointed with the Holy Spirit, to be our chief Prophet and Teacher, fully revealing to us the secret purpose and will of God concerning our redemption; to be our only High Priest, having redeemed us by the one sacrifice of his body and ever interceding for us with the Father; and to be our eternal King, governing us by His Word and Spirit, and defending us and sustaining us in the redemption he has won for us.

> "Q. 32. But why are you called a Christian?
> A.   Because through faith I share in Christ and thus in his

> anointing, so that I may confess his name, offer myself
> a living sacrifice of gratitude to him, and fight against
> sin and the devil and with a free and good conscious
> throughout this life and hereafter rule with him, in
> eternity over all creatures.

It was in the cosmopolitan but corrupt environment of Syrian Antioch that persons committed to Christ were first called *Christians* (Acts 11:26). Are we living up to our name in the context of this crooked and depraved generation, shining like stars in the universe, holding out the word of life, by the anointing of the Spirit of Christ?

---

1. Abraham Kuyper, *The Work of the Holy Spirit*, p. 94.

2. N. B. Stonehouse, *The Witness of Luke to Christ* (Grand Rapids: Eerdmans, 1951), p. 80.

3. John Calvin, *Commentary on a Harmony of the Evangelists, Matthew, Mark, and Luke*, trans. William Pringle, 3 vols. (Edinburgh: Calvin Translation Society, 1845-46), 1:229 (on Luke 4:18).

4. Matthew Henry, *An Exposition of the Old and New Testament*, 9 vols. (London: Nisbet, 1857), 7:624 (on Luke 4:18).

5. Calvin, *Harmony of the Evangelists*, 1:229 (on Luke 4:18).

6. Alfred Plummer, *Commentary on the Gospel According to St. Luke*, 5th ed., The International Critical Commentary on the Holy Scriptures of the Old and New Testaments (London: T. & T. Clark, 1922), p. 122 (on Luke 4:19).

7. Norval Geldenhuys, *Commentary on the Gospel of Luke*, The New International Commentary on the New Testament (Grand Rapids: Eerdmans, 1952), p. 166 (on Luke 4:19).

8. Stonehouse, *Witness of Luke to Christ*, p. 68.

9. John Owen, *A Discourse Concerning the Holy Spirit*, p. 331.

5

SECRET OF SACRED JOY

Luke 10:21-24

We often think of Jesus as the man of sorrows and acquainted with grief. The Suffering Servant prophetically portrayed by Isaiah is the same person described in the gospels as no stranger to sadness. He weeps at the grave of a friend like Lazarus, experiences anguish of soul in the Garden of Gethsemane, sheds tears over the impenitent city of Jerusalem. Yet Christ could also go to a wedding feast in Cana and share in the joy of the occasion by turning water into wine. He knows moments of spiritual ecstasy and expresses sacred joy when deeply moved by the Holy Spirit.

The same Spirit who put joy in the heart of Christ gives gladness to the Christian. For real joy is the fruit of the Spirit.

The Joyful Christ

There is joy in the heart of Jesus, created and sustained by the Holy Spirit. For the fruit of the Spirit is not only "love . . . peace, patience, kindness, goodness, faithfulness, gentleness and self-control," but it is also "joy" (Gal. 5:22, 23).

The joy of the Spirit in Jesus is related to the reality of revelation. It is written that "full of joy through the Holy Spirit,"

Jesus said: "I praise you, Father, Lord of heaven and earth, because you have hidden these things from the wise and learned, and revealed them to little children. Yes, Father, for this was your good pleasure." Then Jesus continued: "All things have been committed to me by my Father. No one knows who the Son is except the Father, and no one knows who the Father is except the Son and those to whom the Son chooses to reveal him. . . . Blessed are the eyes that see what you see. For I tell you that many prophets and kings wanted to see what you see but did not see it, and to hear what you hear but did not hear it" (Luke 10:21-24).

In these verses, Jesus joyfully acknowledged the "Father, Lord of heaven and earth." He expresses a "joyful and confident acquiescence in the ways of God."[1] The Lord of heaven and earth has sovereign authority and power to dispose as He ordains. The Almighty has justly "hidden" the gospel truth from those who refuse to listen when He speaks and shut their eyes to what He reveals. He does not cast pearls before swine. They may know much about science and finance or be skilled in law or literature, but if they remain proud, conceited, and opinionated, then the truth of God is hidden from the eyes of their understanding. They shall miss the one sure way to the forgiveness of sins and the life everlasting until they become as little children and are willing to let the Lord show them the way.

The Father of grace, mercy, compassion, and lovingkindness is most willing to reveal the gospel truth to "little children." He demonstrates His "good pleasure" in disclosing to the teachable mind and responsive will His saving truth. The Father delights to make known the wonders of His grace to the humble in heart. He gives them understanding because "in child-like simplicity and humility they feel their utter dependence on the Lord and accept without intellectual arrogance the truths revealed by God."[2] What He justly withholds from the proud, He graciously shares with the humble. Fishermen and tax collectors who are willing to listen learn what Pharisees and Sadducees can never grasp until they, too, come to the place of commitment. Surren-

der to His will is the condition of knowing the truth that makes
men free. Surely, the God of majesty and mercy fills the hungry
with good things but sends the rich away empty (Luke 1:53).

If, in a "state of spiritual ecstasy" Jesus acknowledged the
Father and Lord who hides or reveals the gospel truth according
to His will,[3] He also affirmed His uniqueness as the revealer of
the unseen God. Jesus joyfully declares that the Son is known by
the Father, and the Father is known by the Son in a most inti-
mate, comprehensive, exclusive way. The Father makes known
the Son, and the Son makes known the Father.

Jesus, by this extraordinary affirmation, gives "unambiguous
testimony to His unity with the Father. The Father has given
everything over to Him; He alone knows the Father in an abso-
lute sense; and only through Him can anyone come to know the
Father. Not only does the Son know the Father, but He is able to
reveal Him to others, so that it follows that He is absolutely one
with the Father."[4] In this affirmation, we can hear "an echo of
the joys of His eternal generation."[5]

To see the Son with eyes of faith is to behold "the light of the
gospel of the glory of Christ, who is the image of God" and "the
light of the knowledge of the glory of God in the face of Christ" (II
Cor. 4:5, 6). To contemplate Jesus Christ as He is portrayed in the
Scriptures is to encounter the invisible God (John 1:18; 14:9; Col.
1:15; Heb. 1:1-3).

The Spirit-filled Jesus, having acknowledged the sovereignty
of God and affirmed His uniqueness in revealing the Father, also
assured the disciples of their high privilege in Luke 10:23, 24.
Prophets and kings, in ages past, had a messianic hope. Moses
looked for the coming of the great prophet who would infallibly
communicate the heart and mind of God to His people (Deut.
18:15). David predicted the advent of the supreme king whose
righteous realm would go from sea to sea and bring an abundance of peace to His people (Ps. 72). Isaiah foretold the appearing of a servant who would be absolutely faithful to God and
suffer sacrificially for the sins of others (Isa. 53). But Moses,
David, and Isaiah, like so many others who lived in hope, did

not see the fulfillment of the promises. But now God's word has been kept. Prophecy has matured into history. The disciples have been privileged to see and hear what others deeply desired but did not live to experience. They have thus received a blessing "not given to any previous generation."[6] Today, confronted with God's final revelation in Christ and the completed Scriptures of the Old and New Testaments, we are also numbered among the highly privileged. Have we truly received the gospel? And if we have been transformed by its truth, are we faithfully transmitting it to others?

We know from what is written elsewhere in the New Testament that the joy of Jesus is related not only to the reality of revelation but also to the accomplishment of redemption. Christ, who is "The Pioneer and Perfecter of our faith," shows us how to persevere in the Christian life. "For the joy set before him," Jesus "endured the cross, scorning its shame," and is now enthroned in the place of divine majesty (Heb. 12:2).

The Holy Spirit produced joy in the heart of Jesus, so that He was enabled to endure the opposition of sinful men and suffer even the death of the cross. The Spirit showed Him the vision of what His atonement would accomplish. The Spirit kept before His eyes the promise that His suffering and sacrifice would be followed by satisfaction. After the cross, the crown. After the pain, the gain. He would certainly see the result of the travail of His soul and be satisfied. His death was not destined to be in vain but would accomplish the divine purpose and achieve the redemption of His people from the penalty and power of sin (Isa. 53:11).

The Joyful Christian

As the Spirit produced real joy in Jesus Christ, so He puts genuine gladness into the life of the Christian. "The fruit of the Spirit is . . . joy" (Gal. 5:22). And that joy is related to the person and work of Christ. For the Spirit causes us to rejoice as He takes the things of Christ and makes them known to us. He gives us joy by applying to our hearts the blessings won for us by Jesus.

Think, first, of the incarnation of Christ. This great event is cause for rejoicing, and the Spirit who speaks in the Scriptures reminds us of it that we may be glad. Abraham rejoiced at the thought of Messiah's advent (John 8:56). John the Baptist, while yet in the womb of Elizabeth, "leaped for joy" in the presence of the unborn Jesus (Luke 1:44). And Mary rejoiced in God her Saviour, contemplating the wonder of the incarnation (Luke 1:47). The wise men who journeyed from the east were "over-joyed" when they saw the star which would bring them to the newborn King (Matt. 2:10). Ought not we to rejoice at "the mystery of godliness" (I Tim. 3:16)? In Jesus Christ, God was made manifest to deal decisively and graciously with our sin.

The Spirit also gladdens us by recalling the fact of the resurrection of Christ. As the disciples were discouraged because of the death of Jesus, so they were made glad by the presence of the living Christ (John 20:20). Let the eyes of faith behold the wounds of redeeming love in His hands and side, let faith see the risen Lord in all His power, then every believer will experience the joy of those disciples recounted in the gospels. Death has been defeated. The Christ of the cross is no crucifix. He is alive. And because He lives, we too shall live (John 14:19).

The joy which the Holy Spirit brings us is related to Christ's salvation. He opens our hearts to receive God's word of good news with gladness (Matt. 13:44). The Christians of the Macedonian seaport of Thessalonica knew that the gospel came to them in a powerfully persuasive way, "with the Holy Spirit and with deep conviction," so that they "welcomed the message with the joy given by the Holy Spirit" (I Thess. 1:5, 6). The people of Samaria received the gospel and trusted in Christ, so that "there was great joy" in their city (Acts 8:8). And the Ethiopian nobleman, evangelized by Philip, "went on his way rejoicing" (Acts 8:39).

The joy of salvation, wrought by the Spirit who relates us to Christ, endures even in the face of difficulties. Persecuted, the apostles nevertheless rejoiced "because they had been counted worthy of suffering disgrace for the Name" (Acts 5:41). And the Christians of Pisidian Antioch, bereft of Paul and Barnabas

when a mob drove them from the city, were still "filled with joy
and with the Holy Spirit" (Acts 13:52). The Spirit assured them of
pardon for sin and peace with God through faith in Christ, and
thus gladdened them with a solid and lasting joy. When the
Spirit speaks to us in the Scriptures of the salvation Christ has
achieved for His people and we believe the gospel, we shall
experience the same joy.

The Spirit makes us rejoice by pointing us to the glorification
of Christ. The head of Jesus, once crowned with thorns, is
crowned with glory now. Jesus Christ is Lord. Someday,
everyone who has served Christ faithfully shall hear Him say,
"Come and share your master's happiness" (Matt. 25:21, 23).
With such a prospect in view, the apostle Paul once said, "I
consider my life worth nothing to me, if only I may finish the race
and complete the task the Lord Jesus has given me—the task of
testifying to the gospel of God's grace" (Acts 20:24). We have
great expectations. We look forward to being with Christ and
being like Christ in His glory. Thus we can be "joyful in hope,
patient in affliction, faithful in prayer" (Rom. 12:12). The Spirit
who points us to the returning Lord encourages us to "rejoice in
the hope of the glory of God." This hope shall not fail. We are
sure that it will be realized "because God has poured out his love
into our hearts by the Holy Spirit, whom he has given us" (Rom.
5:2, 5).

In this world, we shall experience tribulation. God's children
are not immune to sickness, suffering, and sorrow. But ahead is
the blessedness which God has prepared for them that love Him.
Here and now, we pass through difficulty and distress. Yet we
lift up our hearts and look for the return of our glorious Lord.
Though we have not seen Him as the disciples did in Judea and
Galilee, yet we love Him. And we believe in Him. Such faith and
love, stirred by the Spirit, fill us "with an inexpressible and
glorious joy" (I Peter 1:8).

Satan, the old serpent, hisses a message designed to drive us
into despondency and depression. He sows the seeds of doubt
and discouragement, so that like thorns and thistles they spring

up to choke the flowers of hope and joy. But the Spirit still speaks in the Scripture given by His divine inspiration. Through the imprisoned apostle, He commands us, "Rejoice in the Lord always" (Phil. 4:4). God is for us. God is with us. And we shall be with Christ in glory.

"May the God of hope fill you with great joy and peace as you trust in him, so that you may overflow with hope by the power of the Holy Spirit" (Rom. 15:13). Look beyond this time of testing and this vale of tears. The best is yet to be. "To him who is able to keep you from falling and to present you before his glorious presence without fault and with great joy—to the only God our Savior be glory, majesty, power and authority, through Jesus Christ our Lord, before all ages, now and forevermore! Amen" (Jude 24, 25).

---

1. Frederick Godet, *Commentary on the Gospel of Luke*, trans. E. W. Shalders, 4th ed. (1890; reprint ed., 2 vols. in 1, Classic Commentary Library, Grand Rapids: Zondervan, n.d.), 2:28 (on Luke 10:21).

2. Norval Geldenhuys, *Commentary on the Gospel of Luke*, The New International Commentary on the New Testament (Grand Rapids: Eerdmans, 1952), p. 306 (on Luke 10:21).

3. W. F. Arndt, *The Gospel According to St. Luke* (St. Louis: Concordia, 1956), p. 286 (on Luke 10:21).

4. Geldenhuys, *Gospel of Luke*, p. 307 (on Luke 10:22).

5. Godet, *Gospel of Luke*, 2:29 (on Luke 10:22).

6. Leon Morris, *The Gospel According to St. Luke*, The Tyndale New Testament Commentaries (Grand Rapids: Eerdmans, 1974), p. 187 (on Luke 10:23f.).

6

JESUS: DAVID'S SON
OR SATAN'S SON?

Matthew 12:22-32

What do we think of Jesus? Is He the Son of David, the promised Messiah, the world's Saviour? Or is He an impostor, a false Christ, acting in collusion with the world's oppressor, Satan himself? These are the two ultimate alternatives, and we must choose between them. Neutrality is entirely out of the question.

Driving Out Demons

Matthew recalls how one day some concerned friends brought "a demon-possessed man who was blind and mute" to Jesus (12:22). Satan and the demons who serve him were especially active during Christ's work on earth, confronting Jesus and opposing His ministry among men.

Consider this man who was blind and mute. See in him the likeness of many who, in a spiritual sense, are stricken blind and dumb. Under the influence of Satan, they are blind to their personal predicament as sinners. They cannot see their condemnation and corruption, nor do they discern the willingness of God to forgive them and give them a new life in Christ. They fail to perceive Jesus as the Saviour from sin's penalty and power. They are blind to the glory of Christ revealed in the gospel (II Cor. 4:3-6). And they are mute, insofar as confessing the guilt of their sins or acknowledging the lordship of Christ is concerned. Of course, they have eyes to covet what belongs to others. They see the achievements of others and are jealous. They use their tongues to speak untruths and even curse the name of Jesus Christ. But they are stricken blind and dumb with regard to an awareness of God and a meaningful response to Him.

The good news is that when Jesus met this demon-possessed man, He healed him. The evidence of this wonderful healing was evident in the fact that "he could both talk and see" (Matt. 12:22). Jesus caused him to experience a miraculous recovery of sight and speech. If the Bible tells of "the reality of temptation and rebellion, of resistance and disobedience, of confusion and destruction" due to Satan and the demonic, it also makes plain the truth that all this is "a reality over which God is surely triumphant" through the work of Christ.[1] There is deliverance through Him. He "casts out devils in such a manner as to restore to God the men in whom they dwelt, sound and whole."[2]

Paul prays that we may be liberated from sightlessness of soul. He keeps asking "that the God of our Lord Jesus Christ, the glorious Father, may give you the Spirit of wisdom and revelation, so that you may know him better. I pray also that the eyes of your heart may be enlightened in order that you may know . . ." (Eph. 1:17, 18). By the mighty grace of Christ, we are delivered from spiritual blindness and behold "the light of the knowledge of the glory of God in the face of Christ" (II Cor. 4:6). We begin to see the moral excellence of Jesus, to behold the beauty of the Lord who saves, and we entrust ourselves wholeheartedly to Him. We also discern duties long ignored and resolve by His grace to fulfill our responsibilities in the family, the church, the neighborhood, and the nation to the glory of God.

Are we stricken dumb, so that we can neither confess our faults nor give God thanks? In Christ is the help we need. He loosens the tongue of the dumb, so that we are free to sing the

Lord's praise and bold to bear witness to Him who has made us whole. Aware of our need and confident of His power to deliver us, we are personally encouraged by the psalmist to pray, "O Lord, open thou my lips; and my mouth shall shew forth thy praise" (Ps. 51:15). Then alone shall the words of our mouths, like the meditations of our hearts, be acceptable in the sight of Him who is our Strength and our Redeemer.

The miracle wrought by Jesus caused the people to marvel. In their amazement, they began to ask, "Could this be the Son of David?" (Matt. 12:23). Was this the promised Messiah, of whom the prophets foretold in ancient Scripture? Prophesying of the blessings to be experienced in the messianic era, Isaiah had said: "Then the eyes of the blind shall be opened, and the ears of the deaf shall be unstopped. Then shall the lame man leap as an hart, and the tongue of the dumb sing" (35:5, 6). If this Jesus of Nazareth actually does what the prophet promised, is He not the fulfillment of that messianic promise? Is He not the Son of David, the Messiah for whose coming we have waited so long?

The mighty works of Jesus are not only signs of His loving-kindness and compassion for men in misery, but credentials in support of His claim to be the Christ. His works accompany and authenticate His words. We are called to believe in Him therefore, not only because of what He says, but also because of what He does. His works are His credentials, solid evidence that He is the One who should come. The Messiah is here. We need not, we must not, look for another (Matt. 11:2-6).

While the people responded with amazement and questioned if Jesus was the promised Son of David, the religious leaders reacted adversely and suggested a different explanation for the miracle. They could not deny that a miracle had taken place. But they refused to ascribe it to God's power at work through Jesus. Worse still, they alleged that Jesus was actually in league with the devil. They said, "It is only by Beelzebub, the prince of demons, that this fellow drives out demons" (Matt. 12:24).

Surely, "a diabolical venom must have seized the minds of the scribes, who were not ashamed to slander so remarkable work of

God"[3] by ascribing the miracle to a confederacy with Satan. They could not deny that the blind man now could see and that his dumbness had given way to clear speech. But they sought to discredit Jesus by accusing Him of being in collusion with Beelzebub, the lord of the flies or dung-god of the Philistines, the most unclean of all unclean spirits.

Jesus knew their thoughts. He was aware of what they thought, and He penetrates to the center of our own thought processes. He discerns our hearts and reads us like an open book. "The word of God is living and active. Sharper than any double-edged sword, it penetrates even to dividing soul and spirit, joints and marrow; it judges the thoughts and attitudes of the heart. Nothing in all creation is hidden from God's sight. Everything is uncovered and laid bare before the eyes of him to whom we must give account" (Heb. 4:12, 13). This is true not only of the written Word, but also of the Word made flesh, Jesus Christ.

Jesus refuted their perverse accusation, saying: "Every kingdom divided against itself will be ruined, and every city or household divided against itself will not stand. If Satan drives out Satan, he is divided against himself. How then can his kingdom stand?" (Matt. 12:25, 26). A state warring against itself destroys itself. Such a policy is as fatal as it is foolish. A city deliberately acting contrary to its own interests cannot possibly expect to survive. Would Satan pursue a suicidal course? "How can that which would be folly in a human sovereign be imputed to the most astute and crafty, as well as the most spiteful and malignant being in the universe?"[4]

Jesus continued his refutation, asking: "If I drive out demons by Beelzebub, by whom do your people drive them out? So then, they will be your judges" (Matt. 12:27). That is to say: "You have recognized exorcists who evict evil spirits. You acknowledge that they do this by the power of God. So do I. If you say that I carry on my work in collusion with Satan, then consistency would require that you involve them equally in your accusation. The fact that you accept them but reject me convicts you of partiality."

Now Jesus confronts His accusers with a terrible alternative. "If I drive out demons by the Spirit of God, then the kingdom of God has come upon you" (Matt. 12:28). In Luke's account, reference is made to Jesus casting out demons "by the finger of God" (11:20). The expression goes back to Exodus 8:19 and represents the dynamic, creative power of the Spirit of God. "It is through the power of God that Jesus exorcises demons, and through the potent revelation of His power over Satan and his satellites it has been incontrovertibly shown that the kingdom of God, His royal dominion, has come upon earth and is active in the person of Christ."[5]

We see that it is by the power of the Holy Spirit that Jesus drives out unholy spirits from the lives of men. The Spirit of Christ not only supported His human nature in the wilderness temptation and at the start of His public ministry, but in the performance of all His mighty works as well. As Peter told Cornelius when he evangelized him, "God anointed Jesus of Nazareth with the Holy Spirit and power" so that He "went around doing good and healing all who were under the power of the devil, because God was with him" (Acts 10:38). The miracles of Jesus were "marked by the operation, influence, and support of the Holy Spirit" who "guided, impelled, and animated Him . . . at every step of His messianic ministry." Jesus did not resist, grieve, or quench the Spirit, but "clave unto Him with all the love and energy of the Son of God."[6]

The fact that Jesus drives out demons by the power of the Spirit is definitely an indication that the kingdom of God has actually made its appearance among men. The rule of God over the devil and the demonic has been clearly demonstrated. Christ is the conqueror. The kingdom of righteousness, holiness, and blessedness is a present reality. Its consummation is in the future, but already we may experience a sense of belonging to the kingdom and enjoying its benefits.

The power of Satan has been broken by Jesus, rather than extended by Him, as the Pharisees maliciously charged. Jesus has tied up "the strong man" and can now "rob his house" (Matt. 12:29). His power is superior to that of Satan. He overpowers Satan and proceeds with sovereignty and might to set his captives free. In our conversion, we know this to be so. "For he has rescued us from the dominion of darkness and brought us into the kingdom of the Son he loves, in whom we have redemption, the forgiveness of sins" (Col. 1:13, 14). When the Son sets us free, we are free indeed!

Demanding Our Decision

Far from being in collusion with Satan, Jesus is in conflict with Him. His aim is nothing less than to render the devil inoperative. In this campaign, we cannot be neutral. We are faced with the need to choose Christ or Antichrist. Jesus demands our decision. He calls for commitment. Jesus says, "He who is not with me is against me, and he who does not gather with me scatters" (Matt. 12:30).

You either campaign with Christ against the kingdom of evil or collaborate with Satan to the detriment of the progress of the kingdom of God. You either gather in the gospel harvest through Christian service and witness or scatter the souls of men through the practice of satanic tactics. Calvin reminds us, "they are unworthy to be considered as belonging to the flock of Christ, who do not apply to it all the means that are in their power; because their indolence tends to retard and ruin the kingdom of God, which all of us are called to advance."[7] We must choose. We are either on the Lord's side or allied with the adversary against Christ and His cause. Neutrality in this conflict is impossible.

We are faced with the need to make a definite decision in this struggle. We cannot be neutral. Through Moses, the Lord sets before us "life and good, and death and evil" (Deut. 30:15). If we love the Lord and walk in His ways, the promised land is ours to inherit. Estrangement and distrust and rebellion, however, result in irreparable loss. We either serve the God who made us in His image or the idols we make in our own image. Through Joshua, the same insistent call to commitment comes to the human conscience: "Choose you this day whom you will serve, whether the gods which your fathers served . . . or the gods of the Amorites . . . but as for me and my house, we will serve the Lord" (Josh. 24:15).

Our Lord tells us that there are two ways and we must choose one or the other: either we take the broad way that leads to destruction or the narrow and arduous road that leads at last to life (Matt. 7:13, 14). Ultimately, there are only two masters, and we cannot serve them both. We are challenged to choose (Matt. 6:24).

Paul plainly declares that we must decide between righteousness and wickedness, since these have nothing in common. Light can have no fellowship with darkness. What harmony can there ever be between Christ and Belial? What agreement is there between the temple of God and idols? We are confronted with a call to decision—to a decisive break with all that is idolatrous and satanic, that we may adhere completely and constantly to the Lord God Almighty (II Cor. 6:14—7:1). Far from being in collusion with the prince of devils, Jesus summons men to side with Him in the warfare against the evil one.

Having refuted the absurdity of the malignant accusation made by the Pharisees, Jesus openly declared the enormity of their sin in ascribing His holy work to the prince of devils. Here is one of the most alarming passages in all of Scripture. "I tell you, every sin and blasphemy will be forgiven men, but the blasphemy against the Spirit will not be forgiven. Anyone who speaks a word against the Son of Man will be forgiven, but anyone who speaks against the Holy Spirit will not be forgiven, either in this age or in the age to come" (Matt. 12:31, 32).

The gospel offers us the forgiveness of sins. God is true to His promise and cancels the condemnation we sinners deserve when we express repentance through the confession of sin and put our trust in the Saviour's sacrifice on our behalf. The God of the prophets and apostles is a pardoning God who delights in mercy and grace. But the blasphemy against the Holy Spirit, the dreadful ascription of the work Jesus does in the power of the Spirit to the might of Satan, is unpardonable. Undoubtedly, "To identify the Source of all good with the impersonation of evil implies a moral disease for which the Incarnation itself provides no remedy."[8]

Jesus warns of an eternal sin with eternal consequences. It is far worse than committing a sin against the Son of Man. On the day of Pentecost, those whom Peter charged with the murder of Jesus received the remission of sins and the gift of the Spirit after repenting. But what forgiveness can there be for those who resist the Spirit's action in drawing them to the Saviour? What pardon can ever be in prospect for men who refuse to plead guilty when the Spirit would convict them of sin? What hope of peace can there be for people who show "a persistent and continuous attitude of deliberate and wilful sin against the light, maintained in the face of all God's efforts to bring about a change"?[9]

The truth is that "those who rebel, after that the power of God has been revealed, cannot be excused on the plea of ignorance." Indeed, "this kind of sacrilege is committed only when we knowingly endeavour to extinguish the Spirit who dwells in us." And "God punishes the contempt of his grace" by "eternal judgment."[10]

There is no other sacrifice for sin than the Son and no other power making that sacrifice effectual for our good than the Spirit. "God has provided salvation for us through the blood of his Son, and the influences of his Spirit; and has told us that there neither is, nor ever will be, any other way of salvation for sinful man. Now if we despise this salvation . . . what can be done? We must die, because we reject the only means of life."[11]

Man's conscious resistance and deliberate opposition to the conclusive evidence presented by the Spirit of God in favor of Jesus as the Christ is deadly. For the Spirit confronts us with "such evidence as will be sufficient to condemn, if it fail to convince."[12]

As it is written: "If we deliberately keep on sinning after we have received the knowledge of the truth, no sacrifice for sins is left, but only a fearful expectation of judgment and of raging fire that will consume the enemies of God. Anyone who rejected the law of Moses died without mercy on the testimony of two or three witnesses. How much more severely do you think a man deserves to be punished who has trampled the Son of God under foot, who has treated as an unholy thing the blood of the covenant that sanctified him, and who has insulted the Spirit of grace?" Surely, "It is a dreadful thing to fall into the hands of the living God" (Heb. 10:26-29, 31).

For every sin against the law of God there may be forgiveness upon repentance and commitment to the Saviour. David tastes the sweetness of pardon after the bitterness of guilt over his adultery. Peter experiences the joy of salvation once more after Christ has wiped away the tears of penitence occasioned by his painful denial. But the rejection of the gospel, through resistance to the Spirit who would lead us to faith and repentance, precludes pardon. It is unpardonable.

Yet there is still time to seek the Lord and find forgiveness. And that time is now. The Spirit speaks in the Scriptures and calls us to receive God's pardoning grace. "Today, if you hear his voice, do not harden your hearts" (Heb. 4:7). "He is patient with you, not wanting anyone to perish, but everyone to come to repentance" (II Peter 3:9). "I tell you, now is the time of God's favor, now is the day of salvation" (II Cor. 6:2).

---

1. G. C. Berkouwer, "Satan and the Demons," in *Basic Christian doctrines*, ed. Carl F. H. Henry (New York: Holt, Rinehart & Winston, 1962), p. 72.

2. John Calvin, *Commentary on a Harmony of the Evangelists, Matthew, Mark, and Luke*, trans. William Pringle, 3 vols. (Edinburgh: Calvin Translation Society, 1845-46), 2:68 (on Matt. 12:26).

3. Ibid., p. 64 (on Matt. 12:23).

4. Joseph Addison Alexander, *The Gospel According to Matthew* (New York: Scribner, 1867), pp. 336-37 (on Matt. 12:25).

5. Norval Geldenhuys, *Commentary on the Gospel of Luke*, The New International Commentary on the New Testament (Grand Rapids: Eerdmans, 1952), p. 330 (on Luke 11:20).

6. Abraham Kuyper, *The Work of the Holy Spirit*, pp. 100ff.

7. Calvin, *Harmony of the Evangelists*, 2:73 (on Matt. 12:30).

8. Henry Barclay Swete, *The Gospel According to St. Mark*, 3d ed. (London: Macmillan, 1913), p. 68 (on Mark 3:29).

9. W. H. Griffith Thomas, *The Holy Spirit of God*, pp. 278ff.

10. Calvin, *Harmony of the Evangelists*, 2:74-77 (on Matt. 12:31ff.).

11. Charles Simeon, *Expository Outlines on the Whole Bible*, 8th ed., 21 vols. (1847; reprint ed., Grand Rapids: Zondervan, 1955), 11:375.

12. James Buchanan, *The Office and Work of the Holy Spirit*, p. 27.

7

ETERNAL REDEMPTION

Hebrews 9:11-14

Among the monumental ruins of ancient Rome, near the great Colosseum and the imposing Forum, stands the stone Arch of Titus. Carved into that arch are the figures of Roman soldiers carrying the spoils of war in triumphal procession. The plunder includes a seven-branched candelabra taken from the temple of the Jews at Jerusalem in A.D. 70.

That golden candlestick was once in the holy place of the temple, a reminder of the truth that the Lord is the light of His people. There, too, was the table, whose loaves brought to mind the fact that man lives not by bread alone but by the living Word of God. Across one end of the holy place hung a linen curtain designed to close the way to the holy of holies—the most holy place—where God manifested His presence (Heb. 9:1-3).

While the priests entered the holy place morning by morning and evening by evening in the service of God, only the high priest could go into the holy of holies. He did so once a year, on the Day of Atonement—Yom Kippur. There the high priest brought the blood of sacrifice on behalf of himself and the people he represented, to sprinkle it upon the mercy seat of the ark of the covenant. Then God revealed Himself as gracious and made manifest His reconciliation to penitent sinners by a cloud of glory that hovered over the ark between the cherubim (Heb. 9:4-7).

But now we need no priestly class to mediate between God and ourselves. We no longer present sacrifices for sin. No more are we kept at a distance from the presence of the holy Lord; we are free to share His fellowship. Why? The gospel truth is that full and final atonement has been made. Redemption has become a reality. Like temporary scaffolding discarded when the structure is finished, so the priestly regulations and rituals of the past have given way to the fulfillment in Christ (Heb. 9:8-10).

"When Christ came as high priest of the good things that are already here, he went through the greater and more perfect tabernacle that is not man-made, that is to say, not a part of this creation. He did not enter by means of the blood of goats and calves; but he entered the Most Holy Place once for all by his own blood, having obtained eternal redemption. The blood of goats and bulls and the ashes of a heifer sprinkled on those who are ceremonially unclean sanctify them so that they are outwardly clean. How much more, then, will the blood of Christ, who through the eternal Spirit offered himself unblemished to God, cleanse our consciences from acts that lead to death, so that we may serve the living God" (Heb. 9:11-14).

Redemption Accomplished by Christ

The author of the Letter to the Hebrews bears clear testimony to the sinlessness of Jesus. He declares Jesus to be "unblemished." Already, Jesus has been described as made "perfect through suffering" (2:10). ". . . Tempted in every way, just as we are," yet He is "without sin" (4:15). Unlike other high priests in the history of Israel, who had to offer sacrifices for their own sins as well as for the sins of the people, Jesus is sinless (5:3). "Such a high priest meets our need—one who is holy, blameless, pure, set apart from sinners, exalted above the heavens. Unlike the other high priests, he does not need to offer sacrifices day after day, first for his own sins, and then for the sins of the people. He sacrificed for their sins once for all when he offered himself" (7:26, 27).

Even the unclean spirits concur with this witness to the sinlessness of Jesus. They shrink from His presence with dread, aware of the fact that He is the Holy One of God. An unprincipled politician like Pontius Pilate is compelled by evidence to conclude that there is no fault in Him. The thief crucified at His right hand acknowledges Jesus to be innocent of any wrongdoing. What evil has He committed in feeding the hungry poor, opening the eyes of the blind, enabling the lame to walk, raising the dead, and pardoning the penitent? And a Roman soldier exclaims that the Crucified is a righteous man. The apostle Peter, summoning the testimony to the character of Jesus, quotes freely from Isaiah's prophecy concerning the Suffering Servant of the Lord. He declares that Jesus committed no sin and that no deceit was found in His mouth. When men hurled insults at Him, Jesus did not retaliate. Subjected to suffering, He made no threats. Instead, with the calm confidence of one sure of vindication, He entrusted Himself to the righteous Judge of heaven (Isa. 53:9; I Peter 2:22, 23).

It was not to atone for His own sins, therefore, that Jesus died at Calvary. He died for the sins of others. And He did not present Himself to God in sacrifice under any compulsion or coercion from without, but with the willingness of a loving heart. He was willing to be sent into the world and become involved in our predicament when the time had fully come. The amazing condescension of the incarnation was followed by the even more amazing abnegation that led Him to the cross. He was led as a lamb to the slaughter. Steadfastly He set His face in the direction of Jerusalem, the place of sacrifice. The suffering He would endure there was no surprise to Him, for He plainly prophesied His passion and death (Mark 8:31; 9:31; 10:32-34). Jesus declared the voluntary character of His approaching sacrifice in words like these: "I am the good shepherd. The good shepherd lays down his life for the sheep. . . . The reason my Father loves me is that I lay down my life. . . . No one takes it from me, but I lay it down of my own accord" (John 10:11, 17, 18).

The sinless Jesus offered Himself to God willingly to obtain for us an eternal redemption. He did what needed doing to redeem His people. Jesus paid the price of their release from captivity that they might be set free. The ransom He paid liberated God's elect from the curse and corruption of sin. As sinners, we are subject to the righteous judgment of the King of heaven because we have broken His holy law. But "Christ redeemed us from the curse of the law by becoming a curse for us" (Gal. 3:13). As sinners, we are in bondage to the power of sin. But Christ has wrought deliverance from the power of sin for all who trust in Him as Saviour (Rom. 6:5-12).

We are redeemed, not with the corruptible silver and gold of our righteousness, rituals, or resolves, "but with the precious blood of Christ, a lamb without blemish and without spot" (I Peter 1:19).

Redemption Accomplished Through the Spirit

It was "through the eternal Spirit" (Heb. 9:14) that Christ offered Himself in redeeming sacrifice on the altar of the cross. We do not fully appreciate this aspect of salvation. Our attention focuses on the love of Christ, who died for the sins of His people. We may even remember that it was the Father who spared not His own beloved Son but gave Him up to die for our sins. The Holy Spirit, however, is the forgotten Person of the Trinity. Are we really mindful of the truth that Christ accomplished redemption through the eternal Spirit?

The same Spirit who wrought mightily in the miraculous conception and virgin birth of Jesus, and descended upon Him when He was baptized at the river Jordan, continued with Christ on the way to the cross. As the Spirit anointed Him to preach the gospel to the poor and bring sight to the blind, so the Spirit sustained Him in the accomplishment of redemption.

Jesus prepared Himself for sacrifice through prayer. Thinking of those whom His death would deliver, He prayed, "For them I sanctify myself, that they too may be truly sanctified" (John 17:19). Sanctification is the work of God's Spirit. He sets men apart for service, suffering, and sacrifice. Working in the humanity of Jesus, the Spirit enabled Him to be completely committed to doing the Father's will for the redemption of His people.

With love Jesus went to the place of sacrifice. He told the disciples: "No one has greater love than the one who lays down his life for his friends. You are my friends . . ." (John 15:13, 14). The apostle Paul could look back to Calvary and say, "The Son of God . . . loved me and gave himself for me" (Gal. 2:20). The compassionate concern of Jesus, the redemptive love of the Saviour, was the evidence of the Spirit's presence in His humanity. For "the fruit of the Spirit is love" (Gal. 5:22).

Our Lord went to the cross with an attitude of obedience to the Father's will. He was submissive, willing to see the Scriptures fulfilled, no matter what the cost. Jesus delighted in doing the Father's will. With passionate intensity He moved to the place of sacrifice. As He obeyed the precepts of God's law, so He endured the penalties of that law on behalf of His people, willingly. Such obedience was a sign of the Spirit within. For while the unspiritual mind ignores God's claims and rebels against His orders, the Spirit inclines the soul to do His will (Rom. 8:5-8).

Even in desolation, Jesus kept trusting in the Father. On the cross, He prayed to the Father for the forgiveness of those who were ignorantly crucifying the Lord of glory (Luke 23:34). At the last, He confidently committed His spirit into His Father's hands (Luke 23:46). And even when He uttered that cry of abandonment, it was "my God, my God" to whom He cried (Matt. 27:46). Surely, His unwavering trust shows the reality of the Spirit of faith in the crucified Christ (II Cor. 4:13).

We are told that it was "for the joy set before him" that Jesus "endured the cross, scorning its shame" (Heb. 12:2). Who could create and sustain such joy in the heart of Jesus as He approached the agony and anguish of atonement, but the Spirit of God? (Gal. 5:22).

It was through the eternal Spirit that Jesus accomplished redemption. "The Son was willing so to empty Himself that it would be possible for His human nature to pass through eternal death; and to this end He let it be filled with the mightiness of the Spirit of God." The Spirit "enabled Him to finish that eternal work of satisfaction whereby our souls are redeemed."[1]

Redemption Accomplished for Us

We know from the gospel that Christ endured the agony of Gethsemane, the ignominy of arrest, the pain of betrayal and denial, the shame of spitting and scourging, the bitterness of vinegar, and the sharpness of thorns in order to obtain eternal redemption for us.

Rightly we affirm the vicarious aspect of the voluntary sacrifice of Jesus on the cross. "He was wounded for our transgressions, he was bruised for our iniquities: the chastisement of our peace was upon him; and with his stripes we are healed. All we like sheep have gone astray; we have turned every one to his own way; and the Lord hath laid on him the iniquity of us all" (Isa. 53:5, 6).

The gospel truth is that "God made him who had no sin to be sin for us, so that in him we might become the righteousness of God" (II Cor. 5:21). ". . . Christ died for our sins according to the Scriptures" (I Cor. 15:3). "He is the atoning sacrifice for our sins . . ." (I John 2:2). "He himself bore our sins in his body on the cross. . . . The righteous for the unrighteous . . . " (I Peter 2:24; 3:18).

What prophets promise and apostles affirm, our Lord Himself declares. "The Son of Man did not come to be served, but to serve, and to give his life a ransom for many" (Matt. 20:28). "This is my body given for you. . . . This cup is the new covenant in my blood, which is poured out for you" (Luke 22:19, 20).

Christ has redeemed His people from the curse and corruption of sin. The blood of Him "who through the eternal Spirit offered Himself unblemished to God" will "cleanse our consciences from acts that lead to death, so that we may serve the living God" (Heb. 9:14).

The Redeemer has died to cleanse the conscience from the defilement of sin. Attitudes forbidden by God's law and actions contrary to His commandments not only incur a penalty, they also pollute personality. But Christ gave Himself in sacrifice to purge our stains and purify our souls. Only "after he had provided purification for sins" did the Son of God take His place of authority and power "at the right hand of the Majesty in heaven" (Heb. 1:3).

"If we claim to be without sin," writes the apostle John, "we deceive ourselves and the truth is not in us. If we confess our sins, he is faithful and just and will forgive us our sins and purify us from all unrighteousness" (I John 1:8,9). ". . .The blood of Jesus, his Son, purifies us from every sin" (I John 1:7).

We are cleansed "so that we may serve the living God" (Heb. 9:14). Our redemption is from condemnation to absolution, from bondage to freedom for service. While we rightly stress the deliverance that comes to us from the penalty of sin, we do not always go on to emphasize the liberation Christ brings from the power of sin. Our insistence on justification should not cause us to neglect sanctification. We are cleansed so that we may now serve the true and living God with a willing heart.

Sanctification has been described as "the immediate work of God by his Spirit upon our whole nature, proceeding from the peace made for us by Jesus Christ, whereby, being changed into his likeness, we are kept entirely in peace with God, and are preserved unblamable, or in a state of gracious acceptance with him, according to the terms of the covenant, unto the end."[2]

Sanctification has both a negative and a positive aspect. Negatively, we are to die to sin. Positively, we are to live to righteousness. As once we served Satan, so now we serve the living God. And all this is related to the cross of our Redeemer and the work of the Spirit of Christ.

The Holy Spirit is Christ-centered. He convicts us of our sins, shows us our need of a Saviour, and leads us to Jesus Christ for salvation (Zech. 12:10; John 16:8-11). He creates faith in our hearts, so that we reach out to Christ and are united with Him. The man who is not indwelt and possessed by the Spirit simply does not belong to Jesus Christ (Rom. 8:9). But the spiritual person knows the meaning of dying with Christ and rising with Him, of dying to sin and living to righteousness.

"If we have been united with him in his death, we will certainly also be united with him in his resurrection. For we know that our old self was crucified with him so that the body of sin might be rendered powerless, that we should no longer be slaves to sin—because anyone who has died has been freed from sin" (Rom. 6:5-7). "Count yourselves dead to sin but alive to God in Christ Jesus. Therefore, do not let sin reign in your mortal body so that you obey its evil desires. Do not offer the parts of your body to sin, as instruments of wickedness, but rather offer yourselves to God, as those who have returned from death to life; and offer the parts of your body to him as instruments of righteousness" (Rom. 6:11-13).

Is the purpose of Christ's redeeming death being fulfilled in us? Have we been crucified with Him, and are we now truly free from the power of sin so that we willingly serve the living God? As the Spirit of Christ resides in us and presides over us, we experience this radical change. "It is He who mortifies and subdues our corruptions," as well as "quickens us unto life, holiness, and obedience." By uniting us to the Christ of the cross, the Spirit renders inoperative "the vicious, corrupt habit and inclination unto sin, which is in us by nature." Let us not, therefore, gratify but crucify the old ego. Keep it "fastened unto that cross where at length it may expire,"[3] so that the new being imparted by the Spirit may live and thrive to the glory of God.

Committed to Christ and surrendered to the Spirit, we experience a "powerful participation of the virtue of the death and life of Christ, in a death to sin and newness of life in holy obedience."[4] "This," insists Calvin, "is the end of our purgation; for we are not washed by Christ, that we may plunge ourselves again into new filth, but that our purity may serve to glorify God."[5]

If a Christian continues to sin, it is not because he has to but because he wants to. The sin which is but the natural expression of the unregenerate man is a clear contradiction of the new nature imparted to man by the Spirit of Christ. The presence of "sexual immorality, impurity and debauchery; idolatry and witchcraft; hatred, discord, jealousy, fits of rage, selfish ambition, dissensions, factions and envy; drunkenness, orgies, and the like" (Gal. 5:19-21) betrays an utter inconsistency between profession and practice in the life of a believer. You cannot claim the blessing of justification through faith in the redeeming cross of Christ and continue a stranger to the sanctifying power of that redemptive sacrifice without invalidating your claim. To be a Christian means dying with Christ to the power of sin and living with Him in righteousness.

This is the plain, powerful teaching of the apostle Paul. What he teaches in the Letter to the Romans, he also declares in the Galatian epistle: "I have been crucified with Christ and I no longer live, but Christ lives in me. The life I live in the body, I live by faith in the Son of God, who loved me and gave himself for me" (2:20). "Those who belong to Christ Jesus have crucified their sinful nature with its passions and desires. Since we live by the Spirit, let us keep in step with the Spirit" (5:24, 25). "May I never boast except in the cross of our Lord Jesus Christ, through which the world has been crucified to me, and I to the world" (6:14).

Paul presents this same truth in the Corinthian correspondence, where our redemption by the blood of Christ is related to the life of service by the power of the Spirit. "Do you not know," he asks, "that your body is a temple of the Holy Spirit, who is in you, whom you have received from God? You are not your own; you were bought at a price. Therefore honor God with your body" (I Cor. 6:19, 20).

The apostle Peter concurs with Paul, relating the sprinkling of Christ's blood and the matter of obedience to the sanctifying work of the Spirit (I Peter 1:2). Moreover, he says that Christ died for our sins, the righteous for the unrighteous, not only that we might be forgiven and reconciled to God, but also so that we might be "done with sin" and live the rest of our lives doing "the will of God" rather than fulfilling "evil human desires" (I Peter 3:18, 4:1, 2).

High evangelical doctrine makes deep ethical demands. It is not enough to preach that we are justified by faith in the Christ who atoned for sins at the cross. We must practice that holiness which is the great purpose our Saviour had in mind when He offered Himself to God through the eternal Spirit at Calvary. May the Redeemer "cleanse our consciences from acts that lead to death, so that we may serve the living God" (Heb. 9:14).

---

1. Abraham Kuyper, *The Work of the Holy Spirit*, pp. 105f.

2. John Owen, *A Discourse Concerning the Holy Spirit*, p. 369.

3. Ibid., pp. 550ff.

4. Ibid., pp. 560ff.

5. John Calvin, *Commentaries on the Epistle of Paul the Apostle to the Hebrews*, trans. and ed. John Owen (Edinburgh: Calvin Translation Society, 1853), p. 205 (on Heb. 9:14).

8

A MATTER OF DEATH AND LIFE

Romans 8:9-11

"It's a matter of life and death." This is an expression we use in an urgent situation. But in the gospel, it is really a matter of death and life. We go from physical death to bodily resurrection and from a mortality due to sin to a new life sustained by the Spirit. Writing to believers, Paul puts it like this: "You, however, are controlled not by your sinful nature but by the Spirit, if the Spirit of God lives in you. And if anyone does not have the Spirit of Christ, he does not belong to Christ. But if Christ is in you, your body is dead because of sin, yet your spirit is alive because of righteousness. And if the Spirit of him who raised Jesus from the dead is living in you, he who raised Christ from the dead will also give life to your mortal bodies through his Spirit, who lives in you" (Rom. 8:9-11).

The Resurrection of the Body

There is a wholesome realism about Biblical revelation. It makes no attempt to hide the fact of human mortality. Nor does the Bible glamorize death. It confronts us with the truth that "man is destined to die once, and after that to face judgment" (Heb. 9:27). The fifth chapter of the Book of Genesis is actually a presentation of this theme with a score of variations. Whether it tells of Adam, or Seth, or Enos, or Cainan, or Mahalaleel, or Jared, or Methuselah, or Lamech, the recurring note is this: "and he died." The only exception in this symphony of death is Enoch, the man who continued walking with God and was seen on earth no more because he had entered into His nearer presence without passing through the door of death.

The apostle Paul refers to the fact of our mortality and relates it to the grim reality of sin. He says that the body experiences separation from the soul in death "because of sin" (Rom. 8:10). What sin? Adam's first transgression. The apostle affirms, "Sin entered the world through one man, and death through sin, and in this way death came to all men" (Rom. 5:12). The virus of mortality now affects and infects the whole human race. Death reigns over us all. Daily, God's word to Adam is fulfilled in his descendants all over the world. "Dust thou art, and unto dust shalt thou return" (Gen. 3:19).

But the Bible does more than strike a note of realism regarding our mortality. It also affirms that our Saviour, Jesus Christ, "has destroyed death and has brought life and immortality to light through the gospel" (II Tim. 1:10). The Crucified committed His spirit into the Father's hands, and His body was buried in the rock-hewn sepulchre of Joseph of Arimathea. But God did not allow the body of Jesus to experience the corruption of the grave. On the third day, Jesus returned from the realm of the dead and gave His disciples "many convincing proofs that he was alive. He appeared to them over a period of forty days and spoke about the kingdom of God" (Acts 1:3).

The miracle of His resurrection is the living center and focus of our Christian faith. It is not peripheral but fundamental. All else depends on the fact that Jesus Christ is risen from the dead. This resurrection means that the Father has accepted His sacrifice for sin and vindicated all His claims. Would God have raised an impostor from the grave? Now we have a living Saviour, a Lord whose sacrifice covers our sin and whose triumph assures our glorious immortality (Rom. 4:25; I Cor. 15:1-21). Surely, "the resurrection is the keystone of the Christian faith. Without it, we have no salvation from sin and no hope of our own resurrection."[1]

The reality of the resurrection is related to the Triune God. It is the work of the Father, the Son, and the Holy Spirit. The apostle Peter stressed this truth repeatedly, contrasting it particularly with the passion and death of our Lord.

> . . . You, with the help of wicked men, put him to death by nailing him to the cross. But God raised him from the dead, freeing him from the agony of death, because it was impossible for death to keep its hold on him (Acts 2:23, 24).
>
> God has raised this Jesus to life, and we are all witnesses of the fact (Acts 2:32).
>
> . . . You handed him over to be killed, and you disowned him before Pilate, though he had decided to let him go. You disowned the Holy and Righteous One and asked that a murderer be released to you. You killed the author of life, but God raised him from the dead. We are witnesses of this (Acts 3:13-15).
>
> . . . Jesus Christ of Nazareth, whom you crucified . . . God raised from the dead . . . (Acts 4:10).
>
> The God of our fathers raised Jesus from the dead—whom you had killed by hanging him on a tree (Acts 5:30).

It is also clear from the Scripture that the Son shared in bringing about His own resurrection. On one occasion, He supported His claim to authority by declaring, "Destroy this temple, and I will raise it again in three days" (John 2:19). We know that this was a reference to His bodily resurrection. And in the familiar passage concerning the good Shepherd who would sacrifice himself for the safety of his sheep, Jesus also said: "I lay down my life—only to take it up again. No one takes it from me, but I lay it down of my own accord. I have authority to lay it down and authority to take it up again" (John 10:17, 18). He makes plain the wonders of His voluntary cross and victorious resurrection.

We must now note the role of the Spirit in that triumphant event. The Holy Spirit, Lord and Giver of life, was dynamically present in what happened on that third day. Although Christ "was put to death in the body," He was "made alive by the Spirit" (I Peter 3:18). Jesus Christ, God manifested in the flesh, was condemned by men to a violent death but "was vindicated by the Spirit" (I Tim. 3:16). The resurrection demonstrated the validity of all His claims to be the Son of God. Jesus was, "through the Spirit of holiness . . . declared with power to be the Son of God by his resurrection from the dead" (Rom. 1:4).

". . . If the Spirit of him who raised Jesus from the dead is living in you, he who raised Christ from the dead will also give life to your mortal bodies through his Spirit, who lives in you" (Rom. 8:11). Our bodily resurrection will be realized by the power of the same Spirit who wrought mightily in the resurrection of Jesus Christ. We are thus encouraged to look for the final liberation, the redemption of the body from the grip of death and decadence. We look for the glory that will be revealed when the Spirit of the living Christ fulfills our hope and we experience the resurrection of the body (Rom. 8:18-25).

Pagan philosophies and sensual practices degrade the body, but Scripture teaches us that it is God's creation destined for resurrection. The body is meant to be the temple of the Holy Spirit, redeemed by the precious blood of Christ, devoted to the glory of God (I Cor. 6:19, 20). It is sustained by the providential answer to prayers for daily bread (Matt. 6:11) and its sexual drive satisfied within the relationship of marriage (Eph. 5:31). While the personality is transformed and the mind renewed, it is the body that must be presented to God in living sacrifice for service and worship pleasing in His sight (Rom. 12:1, 2). And, at the last day, the same Spirit who raised up Jesus on the third day shall resurrect the body of the believer to be a fit dwelling for the perfected soul of the just.

This truth needs to be stressed in our time because of the trials we endure in life and our fear of death. I recall a student conference in the hills of central Italy, near a medieval town whose fortress and turrets tower above the plain, and where the yellow-green flag of centuries past still flies from the tall mast.

One of the young men at the conference, a recent graduate of a prestigious medical school, told me of his fear of death. Although he dealt with accident and disease daily and was no stranger to the fact of death, yet he dreaded his own inevitable encounter with man's last enemy. In our time together, I urged him to think of Christ, who had already triumphed over the grave and given us His Spirit of life. Every believer can now have the assurance of a glorious resurrection. For "if the Spirit of him who raised Jesus from the dead is living in you, he who raised Christ from the dead will also give life to your mortal bodies through his Spirit, who lives in you" (Rom. 8:11).

At the International Congress on World Evangelization held at Lausanne, Switzerland, in 1974, thousands of Christians leaders met from one hundred and fifty nations to pray and plan together for the fulfillment of the Great Commission. Central to the development of this theme was the message of Christ crucified and risen, our only Lord and Saviour. At one memorable gathering, a young girl from Korea thrilled our souls with song. She prefaced her stirring rendition of Handel's aria "I Know That My Redeemer Liveth" with a testimony. Blind in both eyes, she shared with us her faith in Christ and the hope of seeing Him when He returns. This is the believer's confidence, once expressed by another suffering saint. "I know that my redeemer liveth, and that he shall stand at the latter day upon the earth: and though after my skin worms destroy this body, yet in my flesh shall I see God: whom I shall see for myself, and mine eyes shall behold" (Job 19:25-27).

Indwelt by the Holy Spirit, we are encouraged to look beyond this world, to expect the Saviour who will return from heaven, the Lord Jesus Christ. He will change our bodies by the power of His Spirit to resemble His own glorious resurrection body (Phil. 3:20, 21).

". . . For the trumpet will sound, the dead will be raised imperishable, and we shall be changed. For the perishable must clothe itself with the imperishable, and the mortal with immortality. When the perishable has been clothed with the imperishable, and the mortal with immortality, then the saying that is written will come true: 'Death has been swallowed up in victory'. . . . Thanks be to God! He gives us the victory through our Lord Jesus Christ" (I Cor. 15:52-57).

And the Life Everlasting

Belief in the resurrection of the body is a possibility if the presence of the Spirit in the soul is a reality. The indwelling and vivifying Spirit is called "the Spirit of God" and "the Spirit of Christ" (Rom. 8:9). This not only bears witness to the deity of our Lord but indicates a special relationship of the Spirit to the person and work of Christ.

> From first to last, His work is described as carried on in the power of the Spirit of God given to Him. This is that anointing which He had for His office, in virtue of which He is the Messiah or Christ, the Anointed one; and this shows that He is qualified for all the parts of our salvation, not only as God but also as man. He is able perfectly to teach us as a prophet, not merely because He knows all things as God, but because His human mind is enlightened and taught by the Spirit of God; He can appear for us as a great high priest, because He can bear gently with the ignorant and erring, for that He Himself also was compassed with infirmity, and needed the support of the Holy Spirit; He can rule us as a perfect king, because He is not only Almighty God, but our brother, conquering His enemies and ours by the power of the Spirit.[2]

The Holy Spirit is thus called "the Spirit of Christ" since He empowered and endowed Jesus "with all the wisdom, and power, and zeal, and love, needed for carrying out His great commission as the Saviour of the world."[3] The Spirit is also devoted to glorifying Christ in the hearts of men. He comes to remind us of what Christ has said and to make clear the meaning of what Christ has done (John 14:26). He comes to testify of Christ and to strengthen believers so that they also may bear witness to Him as Saviour and Lord (John 15:26, 27). He comes not to focus attention on Himself but to concentrate our faith, hope, and love in Jesus Christ (John 16:13, 14). He convicts men of sin, righteousness, and judgment (John 16:8-11). He leads the contrite to Christ for salvation and encourages them to confess Him as Lord (I Cor. 12:3). He is surely "the Spirit of Christ."

To be a Christian, then, is to be indwelt by the Spirit of Christ. ". . . If anyone does not have the Spirit of Christ, he does not belong to Christ" (Rom. 8:9). Beyond all doubt, we have here "a clear statement that unless the Holy Spirit is within a man he is no Christian."[4] As Calvin remarks, "those in whom the Spirit reigns not, belong not to Christ . . . they are not Christians."[5]

Indeed, Christ dwells in our hearts by faith as we are strengthened with power through His Spirit's work within us (Eph. 3:16, 17). But the Spirit of Christ comes to us not only to reside in us but especially to preside over us. The vital question, therefore, is not "Do you have the Holy Spirit?" but "Does the Holy Spirit possess you?" For the Christian must be "controlled . . . by the Spirit" rather than by his old, sinful nature (Rom. 8.9).

Even after experiencing spiritual rebirth, we know that the old egocentric nature lingers. This we must mortify rather than gratify. To feed the old nature, to fulfill its desires and ambitions, is to displease God and destroy self, but to surrender heart and mind to the Spirit's rule is to discover the secret of real life and abiding peace (Rom. 8:5-8).

Does the Spirit of Christ live within us? Does the Spirit of God prove decisive for our patterns of thought, word, and action? "It is not enough to have some seasons of impulse, some outbursts of enthusiasm."[6] The Spirit must live in us and exercise a permanent, powerful presence over every aspect of our lives. Does the Spirit direct our attitudes and shape our life-style? "What we are governs how we think; how we think governs how we behave; and how we behave governs our relationship to God —death or life."[7]

The fact of physical death does not negate the reality of spiritual life bestowed by the Spirit of Christ. "Although believers die and this fact is conspicuously exhibited in the dissolution of the body, yet, since Christ dwells in believers, life-giving forces are brought to bear on death and this life is placed in sharp contrast with the disintegrating power which is exemplified in the return to dust on the part of the body."[8] The Spirit whose power shall quicken our bodies at the last day sustains our souls all the days of our years.

We enjoy spiritual and eternal life "because of righteousness" (Rom. 8:10). As the sin of disobedient Adam brought death into the world, so the righteousness of the obedient Christ has brought life to all who believe the gospel message (Rom. 5:12-21). And it is the Holy Spirit who communicates this life, "immortal, incorruptible, and unfading to the new creature —that is, to all the redeemed of the Lord."[9]

The great truth is that the very Spirit who raised Christ Jesus from the dead and shall quicken us from the dust is now at work within us (Eph. 1:19, 20). "Certainly the power of God is wonderfully displayed when we are brought from death to life and when from being children of hell, we become children of God and heirs of eternal life."[10]

The life that is lived under the direction and by the dynamic of the Holy Spirit experiences growth in godliness. Only thus do we make progress in sanctification. But what is sanctification? It is "an immediate work of the Spirit of God on the souls of believers, purifying and cleansing their natures from the pollution and uncleanness of sin, renewing in them the image of God, and thereby enabling them, from a spiritual and habitual principle of grace, to yield obedience unto God, according unto the tenor and terms of the new covenant, by virtue of the life and death of Jesus Christ." That is, "it is the universal renovation of our natures by the Holy Spirit into the image of God, through Christ."[11]

Evangelicalism rightly emphasizes the doctrine of justification by faith. We are acquitted and accepted in the sight of a holy God through personal faith in Jesus Christ, the Saviour who has atoned for our sins and earned life for us by His perfect obedience. But is adequate emphasis consistently put on the need for holy living? Do we so feature the work of Christ for us that we neglect to balance the importance of the work of the Spirit of Christ within us? We must experience the Spirit's residence and precedence in our hearts if we would know fellowship with Christ in His sufferings, be made conformable to the likeness of His death, and prove the power of His resurrection here and now (Phil. 3:10, 11). For it is the Spirit who unites us to Christ, so that we are crucified with Him, buried with Him, and raised with Him to walk in newness of life (Rom. 6:4-7). If the Spirit lives in us, then we must count ourselves "dead to sin but alive to God in Christ Jesus" (Rom. 6:11).

True holiness means conformity to the image of Christ by the indwelling power of the Spirit of Christ. As the Puritan pastor-theologian John Owen expressed it, "In the sanctification of believers, the Highest doth work in them, in their whole souls, their minds, wills, and affections, a gracious and supernatural habit, principle, and disposition of living unto God; wherein the substance or essence, the life and being, of holiness consist."[12]

The sanctified life is thus not a sanctimonious existence but a life of union and communion with the risen Lord. It means being Spirit-filled and Spirit-led in the direction of likeness to Christ and obedience to God, according to the Scriptures. It involves the fulfillment of our obligations in the family, the church, and the state. For "a consecration to the Lord without a consecration to our neighbour becomes an illusion or leads to fanaticism."[13]

Living such a life by the power of the Spirit, we find in this world real peace and joy and "receive a rich welcome into the eternal kingdom of our Lord and Saviour Jesus Christ" (II Peter 1:11).

---

1. Ralph Earle, "The Person of Christ: Death, Resurrection, Ascension," in *Basic Christian Doctrines*, ed. Carl F. H. Henry (New York: Holt, Rinehart & Winston, 1962), p. 143.

2. James S. Candlish, *The Work of the Holy Spirit*, p. 40.

3. Ibid., p. 39.

4. E. F. Kevan, *The Saving Work of the Holy Spirit*, p. 51.

5. John Calvin, *Commentaries on the Epistle of Paul the Apostle to the Romans*, trans. and ed. John Owen (Edinburgh: Calvin Translation Society, 1849), p. 290 (on Rom. 8:9).

6. Frederick Godet, *Commentary on the Epistle to the Romans*, trans. A. Cusin (1883; reprint ed., Classic Commentary Library, Grand Rapids: Zondervan, 1956), p. 304 (on Rom. 8:9).

7. John R. W. Stott, *Men Made New* (Chicago: Inter-Varsity, 1966), p. 88.

8. John Murray, *The Epistle to the Romans*, 2 vols. The New International Commentary on the New Testament (Grand Rapids: Eerdmans, 1959), 1:290 (on Rom. 8:10).

9. George Smeaton, *The Doctrine of the Holy Spirit*, p. 75.

10. John Calvin, *Commentaries on the Epistles of Paul to the Galatians and Ephesians*, trans. William Pringle (Edinburgh: Calvin Translation Society, 1854), p. 213 (on Eph. 1:19).

11. John Owen, *A Discourse Concerning the Holy Spirit*, p. 386.

12. Ibid., pp. 468f.

13. Andrew Murray, *Like Christ*, p. 70.

9

TO GLORIFY CHRIST

Acts 2:22-36

Do you remember the first time you heard the wonderful words and majestic music of Handel's *Messiah*? I can still recall my introduction to this masterpiece on the campus of Ursinus College, at the invitation of a fellow student at Westminster Theological Seminary. Like countless others since the premiere performance in Dublin on April 13, 1742, I thrilled to the vibrant notes of "The Hallelujah Chorus" and the triumphant tones of "The Trumpet Shall Sound." Who can hear of Him who feeds His flock like a shepherd or is despised and rejected of men, and not be deeply moved?

In the second chapter of the Acts of the Apostles, we have the record of Peter's presentation of the Messiah. It happened on the day of Pentecost. When men mocked the disciples who proclaimed the great works of God in intelligible languages at the impulse of the Holy Spirit, Peter affirmed that this miracle was the fulfillment of a prophecy made by Joel many centuries before. Then he went on to declare that the sending of the Spirit was actually the work of Jesus Christ. Peter presented the Messiah in a very dramatic way, focusing on His ministry, death, resurrection, and enthronement. From heaven Jesus has poured

out the blessing of the Holy Spirit upon His praying disciples.
The descent of the Spirit is thus the evidence of Christ's exaltation in heavenly glory.

His Ministry on the Earth

In recalling the ministry of Jesus the Messiah, the apostle Peter
"conciliates afresh the indulgence of his hearers."[1] He addresses
himself to those who profess the religion of Israel and claim to
stand in a privileged relationship to the Covenant God. Peter
asks them to hear him out, no matter how impatient they may
feel, no matter how provoked they may become.

To the men of Israel, Peter presents some undeniable evidence. He speaks concerning "Jesus of Nazareth" (Acts 2:22).
Jesus, born in Bethlehem and brought up in the obscure village
of Nazareth, is the theme of Peter's presentation. It is interesting
that the first thing Peter does in the fulness of the Spirit is to
expound Scripture and exalt the Saviour. Filled with the Spirit,
he does not concentrate on relating his personal experience but
puts the focus on Jesus Christ. This is always the way of the
Spirit, to glorify Christ. The apostle refers to the fact that Jesus
performed many "miracles, wonders and signs" (Acts 2:22). The
credentials of Jesus of Nazareth were not on parchment but in the
lives of those who had received the gifts of sight and hearing, of
forgiveness and hope, of love and new life. Confidently Peter
appeals to the knowledge and memory of his hearers, for the
ministry of Jesus was not exercised in secret but publicly. Men
are therefore inexcusable if they persist in unbelief.

Peter not only refers to some undeniable evidence, he also
draws an indisputable inference. He calls Jesus "a man accredited by God" (Acts 2:22). Here was the One through whom God
was at work in the midst of men, displaying His power and pity.
Here was the beloved Son in whom God is well pleased. He has
been attested as coming from God because of His works of might
and mercy among men. Indeed, there were many who saw His
wonderful works and recognized the fact that in Jesus "God has

come to help his people" (Luke 7:16). What do we see in Jesus Christ? What have we personally experienced of His power in our midst and in our lives?

His Death on the Cross

This Jesus of Nazareth, so beloved of God and kind to men, was nevertheless subjected to great suffering. He died the cruel death of the cross. But why did He die? What brought about His crucifixion?

In the death of Jesus the Messiah, Peter sees an event in keeping with the redeeming purpose of God. The wisdom and grace of the Lord has provided a Lamb to be sacrificed for the sins of His people. God has not only permitted the death of the cross, but has also delivered up His Son for our salvation from the penalty of sin (Rom. 8:32). When the sinless Christ died in the place of sinners, He paid their penalty and satisfied the demands of divine justice. The death of Jesus Christ is according to "God's set purpose and foreknowledge" (Acts 2:23). On the way to Calvary, our Lord revealed His awareness of this determinate counsel and foreknowledge of God. He knew that the sacrifice of the cross was the only way of salvation for sinful men. That is why He committed Himself completely to the redemptive task saying, "Not what I will, but what you will' (Mark 14:36). Christ came to do the will of God, even to the extent of the excruciating death of the cross (Phil. 2:6-8).

If the death of Jesus is in keeping with the settled and saving purpose of the sovereign God, it is also the supreme instance of the sinful revolt of men against the Almighty. Thus Peter boldly accuses his hearers of taking Jesus and causing Him to be killed at the hands of wicked rulers.

The sovereignty of God does not absolve men of their responsibility and guilt in the death of Jesus. While it is true that God was in Christ reconciling the world unto Himself through that death of the cross, yet the men who killed Jesus were not interested in fulfilling God's saving plan. So far as they were concerned, they were getting rid of the one who had proven so troublesome to them. They were silencing a voice they refused to hear. They were executing an impostor whose claims they would not recognize, so they turned Him over to the Gentiles to be killed.

We see then that "predestination in its most extreme and sublime form—the crucifixion of Christ—is linked at once with free will and man's inescapable responsibility."[2]

The guilt of those who murdered Jesus was neither caused nor nullified by the determinate counsel and foreknowledge of God. Think of the analogy in the case of Joseph the son of Jacob. His brothers attempted to kill him and eventually sold him to be a slave in a far country. They were certainly responsible for their attitude of malice and deeds of violence against Joseph. Yet through it all God was working out His purpose. In the course of His providence, God led Joseph to a position of prominence in Egypt that was later used for the feeding of the hungry in a time of famine and the preservation of the lives of his own family (Gen. 45:8; 50:20). The truth of God's sovereignty and man's responsible freedom finds expression throughout Scripture. Thus, in the case of the crucifixion of Jesus, those who despised and rejected Him were guilty even though the death of the Saviour was according to the merciful plan of God. "While the wicked sit backward, they row forward to God's decree."[3]

The cross of Jesus Christ confronts us in the gospels and epistles of the New Testament. Although Jesus of Nazareth was accredited by God, yet He was not accepted by men. They despised Him and rejected Him. They caused Him to be a man of sorrows and acquainted with grief. He was wounded and He was bruised. He was crucified and slain. Those who were directly involved in the events leading up to the crucifixion were not acting in conscious and willing obedience to God's revealed will, but rather in deliberate opposition to it. Thus the fact that Messiah's suffering was in fulfillment of God's redemptive purpose in no way removes "the guilt of those who handed Him over to death and carried the sentence out."[4]

Yet there is a way for guilt to be removed. If we repent of our sins and believe that Christ died to pay the penalty for our sins, then the stain is purged and the load is lifted. The gifts of pardon and peace are ours through faith in Christ crucified. This is the heart of the gospel.

His Resurrection from the Dead

The story of Jesus, proclaimed by Peter at Pentecost, did not end with the death of the cross. It moved on to the glorious fact of His resurrection from the dead. God raised the Christ of the cross from the dead, "freeing him from the agony of death, because it was impossible for death to keep its hold on him" (Acts 2:24).

Peter describes the resurrection of Jesus as the breaking of a power. It simply proved impossible for the prince of death to detain the Prince of Life in his dark dungeon. Men crucified Christ, but God raised Him from the dead. It was not possible for Him to continue under the power of death, "both physically, as a condition inconsistent with His Deity, and morally, because the divine plan and purpose made His resurrection necessary."[5]

On behalf of the Christian community, Peter affirms with boldness, "God has raised this Jesus to life, and we are all witnesses of the fact" (Acts 2:32). At the root of this affirmation is an event, a fact, an historical reality. The Lord is risen, Jesus lives. The last word is not with Pilate, Herod, or Caiaphas, but with God. He has reversed the sentence passed on Jesus and vindicated all His claims to be the Christ, the Son of the living God. Victorious over man's last enemy, the Lord Jesus Christ has appeared to His people. He has met them in the city, on the hills, by the sea. He has walked with them, talked with them, eaten with them. They are witnesses of the fact that the Lord is alive after his suffering and sacrifice (Act 1:3).

The Easter faith of the Christian community did not fabricate the Easter story. Until Christ came back from the realm of the dead, the disciples were mired in doubt and gripped by unbelief. It was the fact of the resurrection that created the faith so plainly and powerfully expressed by Peter at Pentecost.

The resurrection of Christ had been prophesied by David the king. In Psalm 16, David contrasted the corruption of the grave with the joy of life in the presence of the Lord. He spoke of resurrection and rejoicing. Yet he did not speak of himself. David is dead, and his body is buried. The words of the king of Israel apply to Jesus Christ, who has been loosed from the bonds of death. The soul of Jesus was not left in the abode of the dead. His body, bearing the wounds of redeeming love, was raised from the grave. Jesus, the Messiah, has entered upon the fulness of joy. In Him has David's prophecy found fulfillment.

David looked down the corridor of the years and spoke of the resurrection of Christ (Acts 2:31). There is no doubt about the prophetic consciousness of David in the composition of Psalm 16. His prophetic awareness, however, like that of others who predicted the sufferings of Christ and the glory that should follow, was not a distinct knowledge of the events which he foretold. The prophets had but "a conscious reference in their minds to the great promises of the covenant, in the expression of which they were guided by the Holy Spirit of prophecy to say things pregnant with meaning not patent to themselves but to us."[6]

The glorious reality is this: the Lord has conquered death and hell. Christ is risen. Because He lives, we too shall live. By the disobedience of the first Adam death entered upon the scene of human history. By the perfect obedience of the second and last Adam, Jesus Christ, has death been utterly defeated. The risen Redeemer has brought life and immortality to light. With Job, believers may confidently affirm that their Redeemer lives. They have the blessed assurance that some day they shall see Him face to face. They know that even though worms should destroy this body, yet in their renewed flesh they shall see God. They look upward to heaven for the return of the living Lord.

His Enthronement in Heaven

The crucified Christ is now risen from the dead and exalted to the place of supreme power and authority. This exaltation, like His resurrection, was foretold by David. He prophesied that the Christ would be a descendant of the royal line and yet be sovereign over all, including David himself. He predicted that the Messiah would be enthroned in heavenly majesty (Ps. 110:1). Now the promise has been fulfilled by the mighty hand of God, for Christ is crowned with glory and honor as King of kings and Lord of lords (Acts 2:33-35).

What Peter proclaimed on the day of Pentecost to the questioning crowd, he also declared in his letter to the suffering saints scattered across a pagan world. The final word, Peter assured them, would not be with persecuting tyrants or mindless mobs, but with the Lord Jesus Christ, "who has gone into heaven and is at God's right hand—with angels, authorities and powers in submission to him" (I Peter 3:22).

The apostle Paul also emphasizes the exaltation of Jesus Christ to heavenly dignity and authority. He tells us that the Father has rewarded the beloved Son for His perfect obedience by raising Him to the place of total power and supreme majesty. To Him belongs the name *Lord,* and all are under obligation to confess Him as sovereign, to the glory of God the Father (Phil. 2:5-11). Christ is now exalted far above every principality, power, might, and dominion. He is head over all things, for the benefit of His people (Eph. 1:20-22). In all things, the preeminence belongs to Him (Col 1:18).

In Revelation, the apostle John presents the glory of Christ in magnificent scenes radiant with a unique splendor. He tells of Him "who is the faithful witness, the firstborn from the dead, and the ruler of the kings of the earth" (1:5). " . . . To him who loves us and has freed us from our sins by his blood, and has made us to be a kingdom and priests to serve his God and

Father—to him be glory and power for ever and ever! Amen (1:5, 6). " . . . Worthy is the Lamb, who was slain, to receive power and wealth and wisdom and strength and honour and glory and praise" (5:12).

From His throne in heaven, Christ sends the Holy Spirit to dwell with believers and give them the dynamic they need to follow His direction faithfully.

On one memorable occasion, a great festival at Jerusalem, Jesus stood in the temple area and said in a loud voice: "If a man is thirsty, let him come to me and drink. Whoever believes in me, as the Scripture has said, streams of living water will flow from within him" (John 7:37, 38). What did Jesus mean by this? "By this," comments the evangelist, "he meant the Spirit, whom those who believed in him were later to receive. Up to that time the Spirit had not been given, since Jesus had not yet been glorified" (John 7:39).

Now, the descent of the Spirit becomes the evidence that Jesus Christ is indeed enthroned in heavenly glory. Only the exalted Messiah could pour out the Spirit upon His people. As Peter affirms in his Christ-centered pentecostal preaching: "Exalted to the right hand of God, he has received from the Father the promised Holy Spirit, and has poured out what you now see and hear. . . . Therefore, let all Israel be assured of this: God has made this Jesus whom you crucified both Lord and Christ" (Acts 2:33, 36).

The Spirit is "the promise of the Father—part of Christ's reward for His obedience unto death, even the death of the Cross. The giving of the Spirit was thus the conclusive sign of God's acceptance of Christ's work, and we should not lose this signification of it. Pentecost was won for us at Calvary."[7]

Jesus had earlier and personally "received the Spirit to the public discharge of His own Messianic ministry." Now, He shares this sacred gift with His disciples "in order that they might continue the ministry which He began."[8]

The Spirit whom Christ sends from heaven is the Spirit of truth. He comes to be with the Lord's people forever. He will teach them the meaning of Christ's words and works. He will remind them of what Jesus has said. He will guide them into an understanding of the truth. What truth? The truth that is God's written Word and the truth who is God's incarnate Son. We look for no new revelations now that the Biblical record is complete but only seek further illumination from Him who is the Spirit of truth. To desire something other than the Word of God written or want more than the Word made flesh in Jesus Christ is to do disservice to the Holy Spirit. For His goal is ever to glorify Jesus Christ by opening our eyes to His excellence as revealed in the Scriptures (John 14:16, 17; 16:13-15).

The Spirit sent by the Saviour is the Spirit of holiness. He enables us to mortify the old ego, implants within us a new life, and helps us grow in godliness, so that wholesome fruit is produced in our personalities to the glory of God (Gal. 5:16-25).

This Spirit is also the Spirit of power. He prays with us and for us in our times of weakness and confusion (Rom. 8:26, 27). He empowers us to serve and witness in Christ's name, even in circumstances of indifference or hostility (John 15:26, 27; Acts 1:8). He personally witnesses alongside us and makes our testimony effectual in the conviction of sinners and the conversion of men (John 16:7-11). He is the Comforter who fortifies us by His gladdening, encouraging presence (John 14:16, 17).

Let it be clearly understood that the Holy Spirit is intensely Christocentric. He does not call attention to Himself. He does not encourage preoccupation with our own religious feelings nor stimulate excursions into the exotic in search of a "spiritual high." He does not divide the body of Christ into believers who are ordinary Christians and extraordinary members of an elite who have had something more than a living relationship with the Lord of the Scripture by faith. He does not allure us to seek Him and neglect the Father and the Son. As the Son came to reveal the Father and glorify Him, so the Spirit has come to make known the Son and glorify Jesus Christ our Lord.

The Spirit, therefore, calls on us to reckon with the reality of the crucified Jesus who is now both Lord and Christ. He confronts us with Christ, that we may respond to Him with repentance and faith. It is certainly never enough to deplore the way others despise and reject Him. And we must do more than admire the costly confession of Jesus Christ as Lord made by believers in the persecutions of pagan Rome or under the pressures of Communist and Fascist totalitarianism. We must personally respond to the Person whom the Spirit presents to our hearts and minds.

Do we acknowledge Jesus as the Christ, our Prophet, Priest, and King? Are we willing to submit our minds to the instruction of this infallible Prophet who instructs us by His Word and Spirit? Are we disposed to acknowledge our sinfulness and accept this merciful Priest as the sole sacrifice sufficient to cover our guilt and bring us peace with God? Are we committed to this King, expressing our allegiance not only in words but in lives dedicated to His glory?

---

1. Joseph Addison Alexander, *The Acts of the Apostles,* 2 vols. (New York: Scribner, 1858), 1:67 (on Acts 2:22).

2. John Gerstner, "Acts," in *The Biblical Expositor,* ed. Carl F. H. Henry (1960; reprint ed., 3 vols. in 1, Philadelphia: Holman, 1973), p. 973 (on Acts 2:23).

3. John Trapp, *A Commentary on the Old and New Testaments,* ed. Hugh Martin, 5 vols. (London: Dickinson, 1867-77), 5:425 (on Acts 2:24).

4. F. F. Bruce, *Commentary on the Book of the Acts,* The New International Commentary on the New Testament (Grand Rapids: Eerdmans, 1954), p. 70 (on Acts 2:23).

5. Alexander, *The Acts of the Apostles,* 1:72 (on Acts 2:24).

6. Henry Alford, *The Greek Testament,* 4 vols. (London: Rivingtons, 1857-61), 2:25 (on Acts 2:31).

7. James Denney, *Studies in Theology,* 3d ed. (London: Hodder & Stoughton, 1895), p. 157.

8. Bruce, *Book of the Acts,* p. 72 (on Acts 2:33ff.).

10

APOCALYPTIC EPILOGUE

Revelation 22:17-21

The last book of the Bible fascinates us. Our imaginations are stirred as we read of angels, beasts, crowns, kingdoms, martyrdoms, victories, whores, virgins, saints, serpents, blessings, and judgments. Above all, we behold the Lamb, enthroned in the splendor of heavenly glory, crowned with many crowns, triumphant over Satan and the hosts of hell. Now we come to the apocalyptic epilogue. How does this wonderful book conclude? It ends with words of admonition, invitation, benediction, and especially expectation. The Lord's people must ever be forward-looking people, encouraged by the glorious hope of Christ's return.

Admonition

The epilogue of the Apocalypse includes a solemn admonition. "I warn everyone who hears the words of the prophecy of this book," says the Lord's servant." If anyone adds anything to them, God will add to him the plagues described in this book. And if anyone takes words away from this book of prophecy, God will take away from him his share in the tree of life and in the holy city, which are described in this book" (Rev. 22:18, 19).

What God has revealed to the apostle John regarding the state of the Church, the conflict with Satan, and the triumph of Christ, now comes to us in "words" that must be heard and a "book" that must be read. God has caused revelation to be written for our benefit. "So long as the Church was confined to a small circle, and the remembrance of Christ remained fresh and powerful, the apostles' spoken word was sufficient. . . . But when the churches began to extend across the sea to Corinth and Rome, and northward to Ephesus and Galatia, then Paul began to substitute written for verbal instructions. Gradually this epistolary labor was extended and Paul's example followed. Perhaps each wrote in turn. And to these epistles were added the narratives of the life, death, and resurrection of Christ and the Acts of the Apostles. At last the King commanded John from heaven to write in a book the extraordinary revelation given him on Patmos."[1]

It is sometimes said that we must get beyond the Bible and the quest for propositional truth to Jesus Christ and a personal encounter with Him. But apart from the written record and its statements of truth concerning Christ, can we ever hope to meet Him and experience a personal relationship to the living Lord? It is only as the Holy Spirit shows us the incarnate Word in the written Word that we may know Him, enter into His fellowship, and have everlasting life.

Most severe is the warning against tampering with written revelation. Beware of adulterating Biblical truth by adding traditions and innovations of merely human origin and passing those off as authentic, authoritative, and virtually on the same level as "this book of prophecy" (Rev. 22:19). Beware of exaggerating one element of what is written and then neglecting other aspects of revelation. Beware of subtracting from it whatever fails to fit the rationalistic filters of a finite and fallible mind. Receive the message as it is written. Don't tamper with it, but treasure it in your heart and act on it in your life. In so doing, you will not only avoid the judgments threatened by the God of revelation, you will also experience the blessings He has promised to all who trust and obey His inspired Word.

On the basis of what is written in this book, and throughout the entire Bible, we confess our faith in the Christ who came and will come again. As He entered this world through the wonder of the incarnation, so shall He return to judge the living and the dead at the consummation.

Invitation

In view of the prospect of Christ's return, the Spirit-filled Church issues an invitation to the unconverted. Here is the word of gospel appeal. "Whoever is thirsty, let him come; and whoever wishes, let him take the free gift of the water of life" (Rev. 22:17).

The blessings of the Biblical evangel are freely offered to those as yet outside the feast of divine grace. The unconverted are called to come, to take steps of repentance and faith, and so draw near in response to the Lord's appeal. They may satisfy their hunger of heart and quench their thirsty souls simply by coming to Christ while there is time. The day shall dawn when the opportunity to repent and believe the gospel will be no more. That is why the Scripture says, "Today, if you hear his voice, do not harden your hearts" (Heb. 3:7). " . . . Now is the time of God's favor, now is the day of salvation" (II Cor. 6:2).

Now, during this moment of golden opportunity, before Christ returns to judge the world, come to Christ and meet your deepest needs. Once the prophet earnestly entreated, "Ho, every one that thirsteth, come ye to the waters, and he that hath no money; come ye, buy, and eat; yea, come, buy wine and milk without money and without price" (Isa. 55:1). Now, the Lord personally invites you and encourages you to come. Listen to His words of promise. "I am the bread of life. He who comes to me will never go hungry, and he who believes in me will never be thirsty" (John 6:35).

Do you sense your need of Him and the forgiveness of sins and fellowship with God which the gospel freely offers to all who trust in Christ? Then come! "There is but one condition—to be thirsty. It is only they who may drink of the water of the river of life and live forever in the life of God."[2] And only they who come to Christ can sincerely and safely pray and sing for Christ to come to them as in the hymn by Joseph Hart:

> Come, ye needy, come and welcome,
>   God's free bounty glorify;
> True belief and true repentance,
>   Every grace that brings you nigh,
> Without money,
>   Come to Jesus Christ and buy . . .
> Let not conscience make you linger,
>   Nor of fitness fondly dream;
> All the fitness He requireth
>   Is to feel your need of Him;
> This He gives you;
>   'Tis the Spirit's rising beam.

Benediction

John's apocalyptic epilogue concludes with words of benediction. "The grace of the Lord Jesus be with God's people. Amen" (Rev. 22:21).

Many of the New Testament letters begin with a note of grace. The following passages are from the writings of Paul.

To all in Rome who are loved by God and called to be saints: Grace and peace to you from God our Father and from the Lord Jesus Christ (Rom. 1:7).

To the church of God in Corinth, to those sanctified in Christ Jesus and called to be holy, together with all those everywhere who call on the name of our Lord Jesus Christ—their Lord and ours: Grace and peace to you from God our Father and the Lord Jesus Christ (I Cor. 1:2, 3).

. . . To the churches in Galatia: Grace and peace to you from God our Father and the Lord Jesus Christ, who gave himself for our sins to rescue us from the present evil age, according to the will of our God and Father, to whom be glory for ever and ever. Amen (Gal. 1:2-5).

The apostle writes similarly in his opening remarks to the saints in Ephesus, Philippi, Colossae, and Thessalonica.

This note of grace is also sounded at the close of several epistles. A few examples are:

> . . . The grace of our Lord Jesus be with you (Rom. 16:20).
> The grace of our Lord Jesus Christ be with your spirit, brothers. Amen (Gal. 6:18).
>
> Grace to all who love our Lord Jesus Christ with an undying love (Eph. 6:24).
>
> May the grace of the Lord Jesus Christ, and the love of God, and the fellowship of the Holy Spirit be with all of you (II Cor. 13:13).

Beyond all doubt, sinners need the pardoning, cleansing grace of the Saviour. And what saint can even hope to exist but for a moment apart from that same justifying and sanctifying grace that flows from the crucified and risen Redeemer? "Nothing should more be desired by us than that the grace of Christ may be with us in this world, to prepare us for the glory of Christ in the other world."[3]

Expectation

The main theme of this closing paragraph of Scripture is expectation. The hope of our Lord's return is lively here. No time is spent speculating whether that advent will be premillennial, amillennial, or postmillennial. There is no discussion of the return being pre, mid, or post-tribulation in regard to the rapture. There's not even any distinction between a coming of Christ for His people and a return of Christ with His people. There is only the grand and glorious expectation of His appearing.

Already in this chapter we find these words designed to stimulate and strengthen Christian hope. "Behold, I am coming soon" (Rev. 22:7). "Behold, I am coming soon! My reward is with me, and I will give to everyone according to what he has done. I am the Alpha and the Omega, the First and the Last, The Beginning and the End" (Rev. 22:12, 13). The One who speaks possesses "the eternity, the immutability, the almightiness, the omniscience, and the faithfulness of the Deity."[4] Therefore His promises and warnings have everlasting significance and abiding relevance. Now we hear these thrilling words of expectation: "The Spirit and the bride say, 'Come!' And let him who hears say, 'Come' " (Rev. 22:17).

Scripture abounds in language descriptive of the Church. Writing to the Ephesians, for example, the apostle Paul focuses clearly on at least three images of the Church.

First, he refers to the Church as the body of Christ. It has many members, each related to and dependent on the others. They function together for the health of the whole body when coordinated by the one Lord, Jesus Christ. " . . . God placed all things under his feet and appointed him to be head over everything for the church, which is his body, the fulness of him who fills everything in every way" (Eph. 1:22, 23). Ministers, moderators, sessions, presbyteries, synods, general assemblies, task forces, councils, priests, bishops, cardinals, and popes whose pronouncements, principles, or practices contradict the will of Christ revealed in Scripture have to that extent succumbed to the spirit of Antichrist. "No human hierarchy has the right to usurp Christ's authority in the church. No secular state has the right to make the church the instrument of its policy. The church dare serve no other master but Christ."[5]

Again, the apostle refers to the Church as the sanctuary of God. Built of living stones brought by the mighty hand of sovereign grace from the quarries of the Jewish and Gentile worlds, "the apostles and prophets, with Christ Jesus himself as the chief cornerstone. In him the whole building is joined together and rises to become a holy temple in the Lord" (Eph. 2:20, 21). All who are related to Christ are thus "being built together to become a dwelling in which God lives by his Spirit" (Eph. 2:22).

Paul also describes the Church as the bride of Christ. Reminding husbands of their duty to love their wives, he refers to the sacrificial love Jesus has shown for His beloved Church. Christ "gave himself up for her to make her holy, cleansing her by the washing with water through the word, and to present her to himself as a radiant church, without stain or wrinkle or any other blemish, but holy and blameless" (Eph. 5:25-27).

Within this Ephesian reference, there is an Old Testament background in which we find Israel portrayed as engaged to Jehovah. The Lord's people are bound to Him in a covenantal relationship (Isa. 54:1-8; Ezek. 16:7-9; Hos. 2:19, 20). The Lord pledged Himself to protect His people and provide for them in redemptive love. They were to show gratitude and render obedience sustained by the strength of a responsive love. We know that Israel often proved faithless to the Lord and broke the covenant. In going after heathen gods and pagan idols that were deaf, dumb, lifeless non-entities, the people committed spiritual adultery against the true and living God.

In the Apocalypse, the bride is contrasted with "the great prostitute" also known as "Babylon the Great" (Rev. 17:1, 5). This unholy woman personifies an ecclesiastical establishment whose social, political, and economic entanglements have compromised its loyalty to Jesus Christ. "Babylon is the world in the Church. In whatever section of the Church, or in whatever age of her history an unspiritual and earthly element prevails, there is Babylon."[6] She is gaudily arrayed, rides on a scarlet beast, claims divine authority over individual consciences and national powers, and persecutes Christ's people on the earth. Finding her lovers among ideologies such as fascism, communism, and secularism, she brings dishonor on the name and cause of Christ. She bears this terrible title: "MYSTERY, BABYLON THE GREAT, THE MOTHER OF PROSTITUTES AND OF THE ABOMINATIONS OF THE EARTH" (Rev. 17:5). She is the church malignant, militant against the saints, "Drunk with the blood of the saints, the blood of those who bore testimony to Jesus" (Rev. 17:6).

Destined for destruction and desolation, this immoral woman and ungodly megalopolis is contrasted with the bride of Christ and the city of God. The Lamb's wife is clothed in "fine linen, bright and clean" (Rev. 19:8). She is "the Holy City, the new Jerusalem, coming down out of heaven from God, prepared as a bride beautifully dressed for her husband" (Rev. 21:2). The true Church looks with longing for the return of the Lord she loves (II Tim. 4:8; Heb. 9:28). In the epilogue at the close of Revelation 22, the Church is again described as the bride.

But the bride's expectation is also that of the Spirit. For the Spirit of Christ, closely associated with the Church of Christ, inspires the cry for the coming of Christ. Consider the work of the Spirit who gathers, governs, and guides the Church from grace to glory.

The Spirit gathers the Church. As He empowers believers to present Christ, so He opens the hearts of unbelievers to receive Christ. But the Spirit does more than regenerate individuals so that they repent, believe, and experience salvation. He also integrates them into the fellowship of the Church. Reconciled to God, they are also joined to one another in the community of faith, hope, and love. To say "the Lord added" to the Jerusalem congregation "daily those who were being saved" (Acts 2:47) is equivalent to saying that "we were all baptized by one Spirit into one body—whether Jews or Greeks, slave or free—and we were all given one Spirit to drink. . . . Now you are the body of Christ, and each one of you is a part of it" (I Cor. 12:13, 27).

The Spirit governs the Church. In his farewell address to the Ephesian elders, the apostle Paul reminds them not only of his ministry among them but also of their pastoral responsibilities. As he has faithfully preached repentance to God and trust in the Lord Jesus, declaring thus the whole will of God, so they must discharge their duties for the good of God's people. He says: "Guard yourselves and all the flock of which the Holy Spirit has made you overseers. Be shepherds of the church of God, which he bought with his own blood" (Acts 20:28). It is the Spirit who thus governs the Church of the redeemed, and men called to rule are accountable to Him for their stewardship of power.

The Spirit who governs the Church not only appoints leaders

through the call of the fellowship, He also equips them for tasks. The deacons of the Jerusalem congregation were men "full of the Spirit and wisdom" (Acts 6:3). Stephen, for example, is singled out as "a man full of faith and of the Holy Spirit" (Acts 6:5). Barnabas, the generous disciple who inspired new hope in discouraged people, is fit for leadership because he is "a good man, full of the Holy Spirit and faith" (Acts 11:24). The Spirit endows the Church with spiritual gifts, meant not so much for personal enjoyment as for social edification (I Cor. 12:14). He indwells the Church and maintains spiritual discipline as the Word of God is trusted and obeyed. His holy presence makes the Church the temple of God (I Cor. 3:16, 17; Eph. 2:20). As the rebellion of the world resists Him, so the indifference and disobedience of the Church to His government grieves Him (Eph. 4:30). May the Spirit ever reside and preside among us.

The Spirit guides the Church. Recall the promise of Christ to His people. "When he, the Spirit of truth, comes, he will guide you into all truth. He will not speak on his own; he will speak only what he hears, and he will tell you what is yet to come. He will bring glory to me by taking from what is mine and making it known to you. All that belongs to the Father is mine. That is why I said the Spirit will take from what is mine and make it known to you" (John 16:13-15). The Spirit is given, not to focus attention on Himself or give us details on eschatology not revealed to the prophets and apostles of Holy Scripture, but to expound on the meaning of the humiliation and exaltation of the Redeemer of God's elect. He guides us into an understanding of what is written in the Word concerning Christ as we apply ourselves to the Scripture and He applies the Scripture to us.

The Spirit, furthermore, guides the Church in carrying out the Great Commission. He not only provides the dynamic for witness, He actually gives direction to the praying fellowship of believers for the fulfillment of the missionary task. The Spirit spoke to the congregation at Syrian Antioch, called for the commissioning of Barnabas and Paul, and led the company of believers to send these servants of the gospel on their way. Thus they were thrust out into the work of world evangelization by fellow Christians and by the Holy Spirit (Acts 13:1-4).

The same Spirit who guides the Church in advancing the gospel also gives His servants guidance concerning when and where they should invest their missionary labors. For example, we are told that "Paul and his companions traveled throughout the region of Phrygia and Galatia, having been kept by the Holy Spirit from preaching the word in the province of Asia" (Acts 16:6). And "when they came to the border of Mysia, they tried to enter Bithynia, but the Spirit of Jesus would not allow them to. So they passed by Mysia and went down to Troas" (Acts 16:7, 8). The Spirit caused them to respond to the vision of the Macedonian who called them into Europe with the gospel. We need sensitivity to the direction of the Spirit, so that we discern when and where to put limited funds and personnel for the furtherance of the gospel. Our plans and projects must be periodically examined in the light of the Word and their relevance to the world, so that we may faithfully follow the Spirit of missions.

The Spirit, moreover, guides the Church in the discernment of sound doctrine. When the purity of the gospel of grace was threatened by those who alleged that simple faith in Christ needed the admixture of human merit to attain salvation, a conference was held in Jerusalem to discuss this crucial matter. After an appeal to the inspired Scripture was confirmed by the undeniable evidence of God's work in the hearts of men, the conference came to a decision. It declared that salvation was not due to human merit but divine mercy, not our goodness but God's grace, not our works but Christ's finished work. And those who arrived at this conclusion did so in partnership with the Spirit. They said that "it seemed good to the Holy Spirit and to us" (Acts 15:28).

The Spirit guides the Church through the words of Christ. In the seven letters of our Lord to the congregations of Asia Minor, we hear the accents of encouragement, exhortation, correction, and consolation. The message of those seven letters, most relevant to our contemporary situation, comes not only from the living Lord but also from the Spirit. "He who has an ear, let him hear what the Spirit says to the churches" (Rev. 2:7 et al). And what is true of the second and third chapters of Revelation is true of the entire Bible. For all Scripture is given by divine inspiration. The very breath of God's Spirit is in the words of Holy Scripture (II Tim. 3:16, 17). God's message, communicated through the sacred writings for our guidance, does not have "its origin in the will of man, but men spoke from God as they were carried along by the Holy Spirit" (II Peter 1:21).

Now the Spirit guides the Church in praying earnestly for the fulfillment of expectation and the return of her Lord. What the Spirit inspires, the Church utters. "We may regard the Spirit as indwelling the beloved community and inspiring it to respond thus to the Lord's promise of His coming."[7] So it is that "the Spirit who lives in the Church, and the Bride that lives in the Spirit, say 'Come!' "[8]

The voice of the Spirit and the cry of the Church are echoed by the individual believer. "Let him who hears say, 'Come' " (Rev. 22:17). Every Christian longs personally for the return of the Lord Jesus Christ. It was a sure sign of genuine conversion that the Thessalonians not only "turned to God from idols to serve the living and true God" but also began "to wait for his Son from heaven, whom he raised from the dead—Jesus, who rescues us from the coming wrath" (I Thess. 1:9, 10).

Together with the Church to which he belongs and the Spirit who indwells him, the disciple says a fervent *Amen* to the prayer for the Lord's return. That we may "confidently do this is the great practical purpose of this book. Where this design is accomplished, there all tribulation, anxiety, and pain are overcome, and there fidelity shall be found to be invincible."[9] The believer says " 'Amen' to all that the Lord has promised; 'Amen' to the thought of sin and sorrow banished, of wounded hearts healed, or tears of affliction wiped away, of the sting taken from death and victory from the grave, of darkness dissipated for ever, of the light of the eternal day."[10]

Come, bright Morning Star, heralding the fresh new day of final liberation from iniquity and mortality. Come, glowing Sun of Righteousness, with healing radiance for all our hurt. Come from heaven, Lord Jesus, and transform the body of our humiliation into the likeness of Your glorious resurrection body. Come, risen Saviour, with the cry of command, with the voice of the archangel, and with the trumpet of God, raising the blessed dead and uniting us all once more that we may be forever with the Lord.

"The Spirit and the bride say, 'Come!' And let him who hears say, 'Come!' . . . Amen. Come, Lord Jesus" (Rev. 22:17, 20).

---

1. Abraham Kuyper, *The Work of the Holy Spirit*, p. 170.

2. Thomas F. Torrance, *The Apocalypse Today* (London: James Clarke, 1960), p. 188.

3. Matthew Henry, *An Exposition of the Old and New Testament*, 9 vols. (London: Nisbet, 1857), 9:826 (on Rev. 22:21).

4. Joseph A. Seiss, *The Apocalypse*, 10th ed., 3 vols. (New York: Charles C. Cook, 1909), 3:473.

5. John A. Mackay, *God's Order* (New York: Macmillan, 1953), p. 95.

6. William Milligan, *The Book of Revelation*, 6th ed. (London: Hodder & Stoughton, 1900), p. 296.

7. F. F. Bruce, in *A New Testament Commentary*, G. C. Howley, F. F. Bruce, and H. L. Ellison eds. (Grand Rapids: Zondervan, 1969), p. 666 (on Rev. 22:17).

8. C. E. Luthardt, quoted in Friedrich Düsterdieck, *The Revelation of John*, 3d ed., trans. and ed. Henry E. Jacobs, Meyer's Commentary on the New Testament (New York: Funk & Wagnalls, 1886), p. 494 (on Rev. 22:17).

9. E. W. Hengstenberg, *The Revelation of St. John*, 2 vols., trans. Patrick Fairbairn (Edinburgh: T. & T. Clark, 1851-52), 2:377 (on Rev. 22:20).

10. Milligan, *The Book of Revelation*, p. 389.

Bibliography

Allen, Roland. *The Ministry of the Spirit.* Edited by David M. Paton. London: World Dominion Press, 1960.

Broomall, Wick. *The Holy Spirit.* New York: American Tract Society, 1940.

Bruner, Frederick Dale. *A Theology of the Holy Spirit.* Grand Rapids: Eerdmans, 1970.

Bryden, W. W. *The Spirit of Jesus in St. Paul.* London: James Clarke, 1925.

Buchanan, James. *The Office and Work of the Holy Spirit.* 1843. Reprint. London: Banner of Truth Trust, 1966.

Candlish, James S. *The Work of the Holy Spirit.* Edinburgh: T. & T. Clark, 1886.

Criswell, W. A. *The Holy Spirit in Today's World.* Grand Rapids: Zondervan, 1966.

Epp, Theodore H. *The Other Comforter.* Lincoln, Neb.: Back to the Bible Broadcast, 1966.

Erdman, Charles R. *The Spirit of Christ.* New York: R. R. Smith, 1929.

Gordon, A. J. *The Ministry of the Spirit.* 1894. Reprint. Grand Rapids: Baker, 1964.

Griffiths, Michael. *Three Men Filled with the Spirit.* London: Overseas Missionary Fellowship, 1969.

Howard, David M. *By the Power of the Spirit.* Downers Grove, Ill.: Inter-Varsity, 1973.

Kevan, Ernest F. *The Saving Work of the Holy Spirit.* London: Pickering & Inglis, 1953.

Kuyper, Abraham. *The Work of the Holy Spirit.* Translated by Henri DeVries. 1900. Reprint. Grand Rapids: Eerdmans, 1941.

Morris, Leon. *Spirit of the Living God.* Great Doctrines of the Bible. Chicago: Inter-Varsity, 1960.

Moule, Handley C. G. *Veni Creator.* London: Hodder & Stoughton, 1892.

Murray, Andrew. *The Spirit of Christ.* London: Nisbet, 1888.

_____. *Like Christ.* New York: Bay View, 1915.

Nichol, John Thomas. *Pentecostalism.* New York: Harper & Row, 1966.

Owen, John. *A Discourse Concerning the Holy Spirit.* 1674. Reprint. London: Banner of Truth Trust, 1966.

Pache, Rene. *La Personne et L'Oeuvre du Saint-Esprit.* Lausanne: Editions Emmaus, 1947.

Sanders, J. Oswald. *The Holy Spirit and His Gifts.* 1940. Revised and enlarged ed. Grand Rapids: Zondervan, 1970.

Shoemaker, Samuel M. *With the Holy Spirit and with Fire.* New York: Harper & Brothers, 1960.

Smeaton, George. *The Doctrine of the Holy Spirit.* 1882. Reprint. London: Banner of Truth Trust, 1958.

Stott, John R. W. *The Baptism and Fullness of the Holy Spirit.* Chicago: Inter-Varsity, 1964.

Thomas, W. H. Griffiths. *The Holy Spirit of God.* Chicago: Bible Institute Colportage Association, 1913.

Tophel, Gustave. *Le Saint-Esprit.* 1899. Reprint. Vevey: Editions des Groupes Missionaires, 1965.

Williams, J. Rodman. *The Era of the Spirit.* Plainfield, N.J.: Logos International, 1971.

Winslow, Octavius. *The Work of the Holy Spirit.* 1843. Reprint. London: Banner of Truth Trust, 1961.

Wisloff, Frederik. *I Believe in the Holy Spirit.* Translated by Ingvald Dachlin. 1936. Reprint. Minneapolis: Augsburg, 1949.

Wood, A. Skevington. *Life by the Spirit.* Grand Rapids: Zondervan, 1963.